THE
PSALMS
OF
DAVID

Isaac Watts

Imitated in the Language of The New Testament And Applied to The Christian
State and Worship

Pacific Publishing Studio

Published in the United States by Pacific Publishing Studio.

www.PacPS.com

ISBN-13: 978-1461087915

ISBN-10: 1461087910

Psalm 1:1. Common Metre,
The way and end of the righteous and the
wicked.

1 Blest is the man who shuns the place
Where sinners love to meet;
Who fears to tread their wicked ways,
And hates the scoffer's seat:

2 But in the statutes of the Lord
Has plac'd his chief delight;
By day he reads or hears the word,
And meditates by night.

3 [He like a plant of generous kind,
By living waters set,
Safe from the storms and blasting wind,
Enjoys a peaceful state.]

4 Green as the leaf and ever fair
Shall his profession shine,
While fruits of holiness appear
Like clusters on the vine.

5 Not so the impious and unjust;
What vain designs they form!
Their hopes are blown away like dust,
Or chaff before the storm.

6 Sinners in judgment shall not stand
Amongst the sons of grace,
When Christ the Judge, at his right hand,
Appoints his saints a place.

7 His eye beholds the path they tread,
His heart approves it well;
But crooked ways of sinners lead
Down to the gates of hell.

Psalm 1:2. S. M.
The saint happy, the sinner miserable.

1 The man is ever blest
Who shuns the sinner's ways,
Among their counsels never stands,
Nor takes the scorner's place;

2 But makes the Law of God
His study and delight,
Amidst the labours of the day,
And watches of the night.

3 He like a tree shall thrive,
With waters near the root:
Fresh as the leaf his name shall live,
His works are heavenly fruit.

4 Not so th' ungodly race,
They no such blessings find;
Their hopes shall flee like empty chaff
Before the driving wind.

5 How will they bear to stand
Before that judgment-seat,
Where all the saints at Christ's right hand
In full assembly meet?

6 He knows, and he approves
The way the righteous go;
But sinners and their works shall meet
A dreadful overthrow.

Psalm 1:3. L. M.
The difference between the righteous and the
wicked.

1 Happy the man whose cautious feet
Shun the broad way that sinners go,
Who hates the place where atheists meet,
And fears to talk as scoffers do.

2 He loves t' employ his morning light
Amongst the statutes of the Lord:
And spends the wakeful hours at night,
With pleasure pondering o'er the word.

3 He like a plant by gentle streams,
Shall flourish in immortal green;
And heaven will shine with kindest beams
On every work his hands begin.

4 But sinners find their counsels crost;
As chaff before the tempest flies,
So shall their hopes be blown and lost,
When the last trumpet shakes the skies.

5 In vain the rebel seeks to stand
In judgment with the pious race;
The dreadful Judge with stern command
Divides him to a different place.

6 "Straight is the way my saints have trod,
"I blest the path and drew it plain;
"But you would choose the crooked road,
"And down it leads to endless pain.

Psalm 2:1. S. M.
Translated according to the divine pattern,
Acts iv. 24 &c.

Christ dying, rising, interceding, and reigning.

1 [Maker and sovereign Lord
Of heaven, and earth, and seas,
Thy providence confirms thy word,
And answers thy decrees.

2 The things so long foretold
By David are fulfill'd,
When Jews and Gentiles join to slay
Jesus, thine holy child.]

3 Why did the Gentiles rage,
And Jews with one accord
Bend all their counsels to destroy
Th' anointed of the Lord?

4 Rulers and kings agree
To form a vain design;
Against the Lord their powers unite,
Against his Christ they join.

5 The Lord derides their rage,
And will support his throne;
He that hath rais'd him from the dead
Hath own'd him for his Son.

PAUSE.

6 Now he's ascended high,
And asks to rule the earth;

The merit of his blood be pleads,
And pleads his heavenly birth.

7 He asks, and God bestows
A large inheritance;
Far as the world's remotest ends
His kingdom shall advance.

8 The nations that rebel
Must feel his iron rod;
He'll vindicate those honours well
Which he receiv'd from God.

9 [Be wise, ye rulers, now,
And worship at his throne;
With trembling joy, ye people, bow
To God's exalted Son.

10 If once his wrath arise,
Ye perish on the place;
Then blessed is the soul that flies
For refuge to his grace.]

Psalm 2:2. C. M.
The same.

1 Why did the nations join to slay
The Lord's anointed Son?
Why did they cast his laws away,
And tread his gospel down?

2 The Lord that sits above the skies,
Derides their rage below,
He speaks with vengeance in his eyes,
And strikes their spirits thro'.

3 "I call him my Eternal Son,
"And raise him from the dead;
"I make my holy hill his throne,
"And wide his kingdom spread.

4 "Ask me, my Son, and then enjoy
"The utmost heathen lands:
"Thy rod of iron shall destroy
"The rebel that withstands."

5 Be wise, ye rulers of the earth,
Obey th' anointed Lord,
Adore the king of heavenly birth,
And tremble at his word.

6 With humble love address his throne,
For if he frown ye die;
Those are secure, and those alone,
Who on his grace rely.

Psalm 2:3. L. M.
Christ's death, resurrection, and ascension.

1 Why did the Jews proclaim their rage?
The Romans why their swords employ?
Against the Lord their powers engage
His dear anointed to destroy?

2 "Come, let us break his bands," they say,
"This man shall never give us laws ;"
And thus they cast his yoke away,
And nail'd the monarch to the cross.

3 But God, who high in glory reigns,
Laughs at their pride, their rage controls;
He'll vex their hearts with inward pains,
And speak in thunder to their souls.

4 "I will maintain the King I made
"On Zion's everlasting hill,
"My hand shall bring him from the dead,
"And he shall stand your sovereign still."

5 [His wondrous rising from the earth
Makes his eternal Godhead known!
The Lord declares his heavenly birth,
"This day have I begot my Son.

6 "Ascend, my Son, to my right hand,
"There thou shalt ask, and I bestow
"The utmost bounds of heathen lands;
"To thee the northern isles shall bow."]

7 But nations that resist his grace
Shall fall beneath his iron stroke;
His rod shall crush his foes with ease
As potters' earthen work is broke.

PAUSE.

8 Now, ye that sit on earthly thrones, Be wise,
and serve the Lord, the Lamb; at his feet submit
your crowns, Rejoice and tremble at his name.

9 With humble love address the Son,
Lest he grow angry and ye die;
His wrath will burn to worlds unknown
If ye provoke his jealousy.

10 His storms shall drive you quick to hell:
He is a God, and ye but dust:
Happy the souls that know him well,
And make his grace their only trust.

Psalm 3:1. C. M. Doubts and fears supprest; or,
God our defence from sin and Satan.

1 My God, how many are my fears!
How fast my foes increase!
Conspiring my eternal death,
They break my present peace.

2 The lying tempter would persuade
There's no relief in heaven;
And all my swelling sins appear
Too big to be forgiven.

3 But thou, my glory and my strength,
Shalt on the tempter tread,
Shalt silence all my threatening guilt,
And raise my drooping head.

4 [I cry'd, and from his holy hill
He bow'd a listening ear,
I call'd my Father, and my God,
And he subdu'd my fear.

5 He shed soft slumbers on mine eyes,
In spite of all my foes;
I woke, and wonder'd at the grace
That guarded my repose.]

6 What though the hosts of death and hell
All arm'd against me stood,
Terrors no more shall shake my soul,
My refuge is my God.

7 Arise, O Lord, fulfil thy grace,
While I thy glory sing:
My God has broke the serpent's teeth,
And death has lost his sting.

8 Salvation to the Lord belongs,
His arm alone can save;

3

Blessings attend thy people here,
And reach beyond the grave.

Psalm 3:2. 1 2 3 4 5 8. L. M.
A morning Psalm.

1 O Lord, how many are my foes,
In this weak state of flesh and blood!
My peace they daily discompose,
But my defence and hope is God.

2 Tir'd with the burdens of the day,
To thee I rais'd an evening cry;
Thou heardst when I began to pray,
And thine almighty help was nigh.

3 Supported by thine heavenly aid,
I laid me down and slept secure;
Not death should make my heart afraid,
Tho' I should wake and rise no more.

4 But God sustain'd me all the night;
Salvation doth to God belong;
He rais'd my head to see the light,
And make his praise my morning song.

Psalm 4:1. 1 2 3 5 6 7. L. M. Hearing prayer; or,
God our portion, and Christ our hope.

1 O God of grace and righteousness,
Hear and attend when I complain;
Thou hast enlarg'd me in distress,
Bow down a gracious ear again.

2 Ye sons of men, in vain ye try
To turn my glory into shame;
How long will scoffers love to lie,
And dare reproach my Saviour's name!

3 Know that the Lord divides his saints
From all the tribes of men beside;
He hears the cry of penitents
For the dear sake of Christ that dy'd.

4 When our obedient hands have done
A thousand works of righteousness,
We put our trust in God alone,
And glory in his pardoning grace.

5 Let the unthinking many say,
"Who will bestow some earthly good?"
But, Lord, thy light and love we pray,
Our souls desire this heavenly food.

6 Then shall my cheerful powers rejoice
At grace and favour so divine;
Nor will I change my happy choice
For all their corn and all their wine.

Psalm 4:2. 3 4 5 8. C. M.
An evening Psalm.

1 Lord, thou wilt hear me when I pray
I am for ever thine:
I fear before thee all the day,
Nor would I dare to sin.

2 And while I rest my weary head
From cares and business free,
'Tis sweet conversing on my bed
With my own heart and thee.

3 I pay this evening sacrifice;
And when my work is done,
Great God, my faith and hope relies
Upon thy grace alone.

4 Thus with my thoughts compos'd to peace
I'll give mine eyes to sleep;
Thy hand in safety keeps my days,
And will my slumbers keep.

Psalm 5.
For the Lord's day morning.

1 Lord, in the morning thou shalt hear
My voice ascending high;
To thee will I direct my prayer,
To thee lift up mine eye;

2 Up to the hills where Christ is gone
To plead for all his saints,
Presenting at his Father's throne
Our songs and our complaints.

3 Thou art a God before whose sight
The wicked shall not stand;

Sinners shall ne'er be thy delight,
Nor dwell at thy right hand.

4 But to thy house will I resort,
To taste thy mercies there;
I will frequent thine holy court,
And worship in thy fear.

5 O may thy Spirit guide my feet
In ways of righteousness!
Make every path of duty straight
And plain before my face.

PAUSE.

6 My watchful enemies combine
To tempt my feet astray;
They flatter with a base design
To make my soul their prey.

7 Lord, crush the serpent in the dust,
And all his plots destroy;
While those that in thy mercy trust
For ever shout for joy.

8 The men that love and fear thy name
Shall see their hopes fulfill'd;
The mighty God will compass them
With favour as a shield.

Psalm 6:1. C. M. Complaint in sickness; or,
diseases healed.

1 In anger, Lord, rebuke me not,
Withdraw the dreadful storm;
Nor let thy fury grow so hot
Against a feeble worm.

2 My soul's bow'd down with heavy cares,
My flesh with pain oppress'd;
My couch is witness to my tears,
My tears forbid my rest.

3 Sorrow and pain wear out my days;
I waste the night with cries,
Counting the minutes as they pass,
Till the slow morning rise.

4 Shall I be still tormented more?
Mine eye consum'd with grief?

How long, my God, how long before
Thine hand afford relief?

5 He hears when dust and ashes speak,
He pities all our groans,
He saves us for his mercy's sake
And heals our broken bones.

6 The virtue of his sovereign word
Restores our fainting breath;
For silent graves praise not the Lord,
Nor is he known in death.

Psalm 6:2. L. M.
Temptations in sickness overcome.

1 Lord, I can suffer thy rebukes,
When thou with kindness dost chastise
But thy fierce wrath I cannot bear,
O let it not against me rise!

2 Pity my languishing estate,
And ease the sorrows that I feel;
The wounds thine heavy hand hath made,
O let thy gentler touches heal.

3 See how I pass my weary days
In sighs and groans; and when 'tis night
My bed is water'd with my tears;
My grief consumes and dims my sight.

4 Look how the powers of nature mourn!
How long, almighty God, how long?
When shall thine hour of grace return?
When shall I make thy grace my song?

5 I feel my flesh so near the grave,
My thoughts are tempted to despair;
But graves can never praise the Lord,
For all is dust and silence there.

6 Depart, ye tempters, from my soul,
And all despairing thoughts depart;
My God, who hears my humble moan,
Will ease my flesh, and cheer my heart.

Psalm 7. God's care of his people and
punishment of persecutors.

1 My trust is in my heavenly Friend,
My hope in thee, my God;
Rise and my helpless life defend
From those that seek my blood.

2 With insolence and fury they
My soul in pieces tear,
As hungry lions rend the prey
When no deliverer's near.

3 If I had e'er provok'd them first,
Or once abus'd my foe,
Then let him tread my life to dust,
And lay mine honour low.

4 If there be malice found in me,
I know thy piercing eyes;
I should not dare appeal to thee,
Nor ask my God to rise.

5 Arise, my God, lift up thy hand,
Their pride and power control;
Awake to judgment and command
Deliverance for my soul.

PAUSE.

6 [Let sinners and their wicked rage
Be humbled to the dust;
Shall not the God of truth engage
To vindicate the just?

7 He knows the heart, he tries the reins,
He will defend th' upright:
His sharpest arrows he ordains
Against the sons of spite.

8 For me their malice digg'd a pit,
But there themselves are cast;
My God makes all their mischief light
On their own heads at last.]

9 That cruel persecuting race
Must feel his dreadful sword;
Awake, my soul, and praise the grace
And justice of the Lord.

Psalm 8:1. S. M. God's sovereignty and
goodness; and man's dominion over the
creatures.

1 O Lord, our heavenly King,
Thy name is all divine;
Thy glories round the earth are spread,
And o'er the heavens they shine.

2 When to thy works on high
I raise my wondering eyes,
And see the moon complete in light
Adorn the darksome skies:

3 When I survey the stars,
And all their shining forms,
Lord, what is man, that worthless thing,
Akin to dust and worms?

4 Lord, what is worthless man,
That thou shouldst love him so?
Next to thine angels he is plac'd,
And lord of all below.

5 Thine honours crown his head,
While beasts like slaves obey,
And birds that cut the air with wings,
And fish that cleave the sea.

6 How rich thy bounties are!
And wondrous are thy ways:
Of dust and worms thy power can frame
A monument of praise.

7 [Out of the mouths of babes
And sucklings thou canst draw
Surprising honours to thy name,
And strike the world with awe.]

8 O Lord, our heavenly King,
Thy name is all divine:
Thy glories round the earth are spread,
And o'er the heavens they shine.

Psalm 8:2. C. M. Christ's condescension and
glorification; or, God made man.

1 O Lord, our Lord, how wondrous great
Is thine exalted name!
The glories of thy heavenly state
Let men and babes proclaim.

2 When I behold thy works on high,
The moon that rules the night,

And stars that well adorn the sky,
Those moving worlds of light;

3 Lord, what is man, or all his race,
Who dwells so far below,
That thou shouldst visit him with grace,
And love his nature so?

4 That thine eternal Son should bear
To take a mortal form,
Made lower than his angels are,
To save a dying worm!

5 [Yet while he liv'd on earth unknown,
And men would not adore,
Th' obedient seas and fishes own
His Godhead and his power.

6 The waves lay spread beneath his feet;
And fish, at his command,
Bring their large shoals to Peter's net,
Bring tribute to his hand.

7 These lesser glories of the Son
Shone thro' the fleshly cloud;
Now we behold him on his throne,
And men confess him God.]

8 Let him be crown'd with majesty,
Who bow'd his head to death;
And be his honours sounded high,
By all things that have breath.

9 Jesus, our Lord, how wondrous great
Is thine exalted name!
The glories of thy heavenly state
Let the whole earth proclaim.

Psalm 8:3. 1 2. paraphrased.
First Part. L. M.
The Hosanna of the children;
or, Infants praising God.

1 Almighty Ruler of the skies,
Thro' the wide earth thy name is spread,
And thine eternal glories rise
O'er all the heavens thy hands have made.

2 To thee the voices of the young
A monument of honour raise;

And babes, with uninstructed tongue,
Declare the wonders of thy praise.

3 Thy power assists their tender age
To bring proud rebels to the ground,
To still the bold blasphemer's rage,
And all their policies confound.

4 Children amidst thy temple throng
To see their great Redeemer's face;
The Son of David is their song,
And young hosannas fill the place.

3 The frowning scribes and angry priests
In vain their impious cavils bring;
Revenge sits silent in their breasts,
While Jewish babes proclaim their king.

Psalm 8:4. 3 &c. paraphrased.
Second Part. L. M.
Adam and Christ, lords of
the old and the new creation.

1 Lord, what was man, when made at first,
Adam the offspring of the dust,
That thou shouldst set him and his race
But just below an angel's place?

2 That thou shouldst raise his nature so
And make him lord of all below;
Make every beast and bird submit,
And lay the fishes at his feet?

3 But O, what brighter glories wait
To crown the second Adam's state!
What honours shall thy Son adorn
Who condescended to be born!

4 See him below his angels made,
See him in dust amongst the dead,
To save a ruin'd world from sin;
But he shall reign with power divine.

5 The world to come, redeem'd from all
The miseries that attend the fall,
New made, and glorious, shall submit
At our exalted Saviour's feet.

Psalm 9:1. First Part.
Wrath and mercy from the judgment-seat.

1 With my whole heart I'll raise my song,
Thy wonders I'll proclaim;
Thou sov'reign judge of right and wrong
Wilt put my foes to shame.

2 I'll sing thy majesty and grace;
My God prepares his throne
To judge the world in righteousness
And make his vengeance known.

3 Then shall the Lord a refuge prove
For all the poor opprest,
To save the people of his love,
And give the weary rest.

4 The men, that know thy name will trust
In thy abundant grace;
For thou hast ne'er forsook the just,
Who humbly seek thy face.

5 Sing praises to the righteous Lord,
Who dwells on Zion's hill,
Who executes his threatening word,
And doth his grace fulfil.

Psalm 9:2. 10. Second Part.
The wisdom and equity of providence.

1 When the great Judge, supreme and just,
Shall once inquire for blood,
The humble souls, that mourn in dust,
Shall find a faithful God.

2 He from the dreadful gates of death
Does his own children raise:
In Zion's gates, with cheerful breath,
They sing their Father's praise.

3 His foes shall fail with heedless feet
Into the pit they made;
And sinners perish in the net
That their own hands had spread.

4 Thus by thy judgments, mighty God!
Are thy deep counsels known;
When men of mischief are destroy'd,
The snare must be their own.

PAUSE.

5 The wicked shall sink down to hell;
Thy wrath devour the lands
That dare forget thee, or rebel
Against thy known commands.

6 Tho' saints to sore distress are brought,
And wait and long complain,
Their cries shall not be still forgot,
Nor shall their hopes be vain.

7 [Rise, great Redeemer, from thy seat,
To judge and save the poor;
Let nations tremble at thy feet,
And man prevail no more.

8 Thy thunder shall affright the proud,
And put their hearts to pain,
Make them confess that thou art God,
And they but feeble men.]

Psalm 10. Prayer heard, and saints saved; or,
Pride, atheism, and oppression punished.

For a humiliation day.

1 Why doth the Lord stand off so far,
And why conceal his face,
When great calamities appear,
And times of deep distress?

2 Lord, shall the wicked still deride
Thy justice and thy pow'r?
Shall they advance their heads in pride,
And still thy saints devour?

3 They put thy judgments from their sight,
And then insult the poor;
They boast in their exalted height
That they shall fall no more.

4 Arise, O God, lift up thine hand,
Attend our humble cry;
No enemy shall dare to stand
When God ascends on high.

PAUSE.

5 Why do the men of malice rage,
And say with foolish pride,
"The God of heaven will ne'er engage
To fight on Zion's side?"

6 But thou for ever art our Lord;
And pow'rful is thine hand,
As when the heathens felt thy sword,
And perish'd from thy land.

7 Thou wilt prepare our hearts to pray,
And cause thine ear to hear;
He hearkens what his children say,
And puts the world in fear.

8 Proud tyrants shall no more oppress,
No more despise the just;
And mighty sinners shall confess
They are but earth and dust.

Psalm 11.
God loves the righteous and hates the wicked.

1 My refuge is the God of love;
Why do my foes insult and cry,
"Fly like a timorous trembling dove,
"To distant woods or mountains fly"?

2 If government be all destroy'd
(That firm foundation of our peace)
And violence make justice void,
Where shall the righteous seek redress?

3 The Lord in heaven has fix'd his throne,
His eye surveys the world below;
To him all mortal things are known,
His eyelids search our spirits thro'.

4 If he afflicts his saints so far
To prove their love, and try their grace,
What may the bold transgressors fear?
His very soul abhors their ways.

5 On impious wretches he shall rain
Tempests of brimstone, fire, and death,
Such as he kindled on the plain
Of Sodom with his angry breath.

6 The righteous Lord loves righteous souls,
Whose thoughts and actions are sincere;
And with a gracious eye beholds
The men that his own image bear.

Psalm 12:1. L. M. The saint's safety and hope in evil times; or, Sins of the tongue complained of, viz, blasphemy, falsehood, &c.

1 Lord, if thou dost not soon appear,
Virtue and truth will fly away;
A faithful man, amongst us here,
Will scarce be found if thou delay.

2 The whole discourse, when neighbours meet,
Is fill'd with trifles loose and vain;
Their lips are flattery and deceit,
And their proud language is profane.

3 But lips, that with deceit abound,
Shall not maintain their triumph long;
The God of vengeance will confound
The flattering and blaspheming tongue.

4 "Yet shall our words be free," they cry,
"Our tongue shall be controll'd by none:
"Where is the Lord will ask us why?
"Or say, our lips are not our own?"

5 The Lord who sees the poor opprest,
And hears th' oppressor's haughty strain,
Will rise to give his children rest,
Nor shall they trust his word in vain.

6 Thy word, O Lord, tho' often try'd,
Void of deceit shall still appear
Not silver, seven times purify'd
From dross and mixture, shines so clear.

7 Thy grace shall in the darkest hour
Defend the holy soul from harm;
Tho' when the vilest men have power
On every side will sinners swarm.

Psalm 12:2. C. M.
Complaint of a general corruption of manners;
or,
The promise and signs of Christ's coming to judgment.

1 Help, Lord, for men of virtue fail,
Religion loses ground,
The sons of violence prevail,
And treacheries abound.

2 Their oaths and promises they break,
Yet act the flatterer's part;
With fair deceitful lips they speak,
And with a double heart.

3 If we reprove some hateful lie,
How is their fury stirr'd!
"Are not our lips our own" they cry,
"And who shall be our lord?"

4 Scoffers appear on every side,
Where a vile race of men
Is rais'd to seats of power and pride,
And bears the sword in vain.

PAUSE.

5 Lord, when iniquities abound,
And blasphemy grows bold,
When faith is hardly to be found,
And love is waxing cold,

6 Is not thy chariot hastening on?
Hast thou not given this sign?
May we not trust and live upon
A promise so divine?

7 "Yes," saith the Lord, "now will I rise,
"And make oppressors flee;
"I shall appear to their surprise,
"And set my servants free."

8 Thy word, like silver seven times try'd,
Thro' ages shall endure;
The men that in thy truth confide,
Shall find thy promise sure.

Psalm 13:1. L. M. Pleading with God under
desertion; or, Hope, in darkness.

1 How long, 0 Lord, shall I complain
Like one that seeks his God in vain?
Canst thou thy face for ever hide?
And I still pray and be deny'd?

2 Shall I for ever be forgot
As one whom thou regardest not?
Still shall my soul thine absence mourn?
And still despair of thy return?

3 How long shall my poor troubled breast
Be with these anxious thoughts opprest?
And Satan, my malicious foe,
Rejoice to see me sunk so low.

4 Hear, Lord, and grant me quick relief,
Before my death conclude my grief;
If thou withhold thy heavenly light,
I sleep in everlasting night.

5 How will the powers of darkness boast,
If but one praying soul be lost!
But I have trusted in thy grace,
And shall again behold thy face.

6 Whate'er my fears or foes suggest,
Thou art my hope, my joy, my rest;
My heart shall feel thy love, and raise
My cheerful voice to songs of praise.

Psalm 13:2. C. M.
Complaint under temptations of the devil.

1 How long wilt thou conceal thy face?
My God, how long delay?
When shall I feel those heavenly rays
That chase my fears away?

2 How long shall my poor labouring soul
Wrestle and toil in vain?
Thy word can all my foes control,
And ease my raging pain.

3 See how the prince of darkness tries
All his malicious arts,
He spreads a mist around my eyes,
And throws his fiery darts.

4 Be thou my sun and thou my shield,
My soul in safety keep;
Make haste before mine eyes are seal'd
In death's eternal sleep.

5 How would the tempter boast aloud
If I become his prey!

Behold the sons of hell grow proud
At thy so long delay.

6 But they shall fly at thy rebuke,
And Satan hide his head;
He knows the terrors of thy look
And hears thy voice with dread.

7 Thou wilt display that sovereign grace,
Where all my hopes have hung;
I shall employ my lips in praise,
And victory shall be sung.

Psalm 14:1. First Part.
By nature all men are sinners.

1 Fools in their hearts believe and say,
"That all religion's vain,
"There is no God that reigns on high,
"Or minds th' affairs of men."

2 From thoughts so dreadful and profane
Corrupt discourse proceeds;
And in their impious hands are found
Abominable deeds.

3 The Lord, from his celestial throne
Look'd down on things below,
To find the man that sought his grace,
Or did his justice know.

4 By nature all are gone astray,
Their practice all the same;
There's none that fears his Maker's hand,
There's none that loves his name.

5 Their tongues are us'd to speak deceit,
Their slanders never cease;
How swift to mischief are their feet,
Nor knew the paths of peace.

6 Such seeds of sin (that bitter root)
In every heart are found;
Nor can they bear diviner fruit,
Till grace refine the ground.

Psalm 14:2. Second Part.
The folly of persecutors.

1 Are sinners now so senseless grown
That they thy saints devour?
And never worship at thy throne,
Nor fear thine awful power?

2 Great God appear to their surprise,
Reveal thy dreadful name;
Let them no more thy wrath despise,
Nor turn our hope to shame.

3 Dost thou not dwell among the just?
And yet our foes deride,
That we should make thy name our trust;
Great God, confound their pride.

4 O that the joyful day were come
To finish our distress!
When God shall bring his children home,
Our songs shall never cease.

Psalm 15:1. C. M. Characters of a saint; or, a
citizen of Zion; or, The qualifications of a
Christian.

1 Who shall inhabit in thy hill,
O God of holiness?
Whom will the Lord admit to dwell
So near his throne of grace?

2 The man that walks in pious ways,
And works with righteous hands;
That trusts his Maker's promises,
And follows his commands.

3 He speaks the meaning of his heart,
Nor slanders with his tongue;
Will scarce believe an ill report,
Nor do his neighbour wrong.

4 The wealthy sinner he contemns,
Loves all that fear the Lord:
And tho' to his own hurt he swears,
Still he performs his word.

5 His hands disdain a golden bribe,
And never gripe the poor;
This man shall dwell with God on earth,
And find his heaven secure.

Psalm 15:2. L. M. Religion and justice, goodness and truth; or, Duties to God and man; or, The qualifications of a Christian.

1 Who shall ascend thy heavenly place,
Great God, and dwell before thy face?
The man that minds religion now,
And humbly walks with God below:

2 Whose hands are pure, whose heart is clean,
Whose lips still speak the thing they mean;
No slanders dwell upon his tongue;
He hates to do his neighbour wrong.

3 [Scarce will he trust an ill report,
Nor vents it to his neighbour's hurt:
Sinners of state he can despise,
But saints are honour'd in his eyes.]

4 [Firm to his word he ever stood,
And always makes his promise good;
Nor dares to change the thing he swears,
Whatever pain or loss he bears.]

5 [He never deals in bribing gold,
And mourns that justice should be sold:
While others gripe and grind the poor,
Sweet charity attends his door.]

6 [He loves his enemies, and prays
For those that curse him to his face;
And doth to all men still the same
That he would hope or wish from them.]

7 Yet when his holiest works are done,
His soul depends on grace alone;
This is the man thy face shall see,
And dwell for ever Lord, with thee.

Psalm 16:1. First Part. L. M. Confession of our poverty, and saints the best company; or, Good works profit men, not God.

1 Preserve me, Lord, in time of need
For succour to thy throne I flee,
But have no merits there to plead;
My goodness cannot reach to thee.

2 Oft have my heart and tongue confest
How empty and how poor I am;

My praise can never make thee blest,
Nor add new glories to thy name.

3 Yet, Lord, thy saints on earth may reap
Some profit by the good we do;
These are the company I keep,
These are the choicest friends I know.

4 Let others choose the sons of mirth
To give a relish to their wine,
I love the men of heavenly birth,
Whose thoughts and language are divine.

Psalm 16:2. Second Part. L. M.
Christ's all-sufficiency.

1 How fast their guilt and sorrows rise
Who haste to seek some idol god!
I will not taste their sacrifice,
Their offerings of forbidden blood.

2 My God provides a richer cup,
And nobler food to live upon;
He for my life has offer'd up
Jesus, his best beloved Son.

3 His love is my perpetual feast;
By day his counsels guide me right;
And be his name for ever blest,
Who gives me sweet advice by night.

4 I set him still before mine eyes;
At my right hand he stands prepar'd
To keep my soul from all surprise,
And be my everlasting guard.

Psalm 16:3. Third Part. L. M.
Courage in death, and hope of the resurrection.

1 When God is nigh, my faith is strong,
His arm is my almighty prop:
Be glad, my heart; rejoice, my tongue,
My dying flesh shall rest in hope.

2 Tho' in the dust I lay my head,
Yet, gracious God, thou wilt not leave
My soul for ever with the dead,
Nor lose thy children in the grave.

3 My flesh shall thy first call obey,
Shake off the dust, and rise on high;
Then shalt thou lead the wondrous way,
Up to thy throne above the sky.

4 There streams of endless pleasure flow;
And full discoveries of thy grace
(Which we but tasted here below)
Spread heavenly joys thro' all the place.

Psalm 16:4. First Part. C. M.
Support and counsel from God without merit.

1 Save me, O Lord, from every foe;
In thee my trust I place,
Tho' all the good that I can do
Can ne'er deserve thy grace.

2 Yet if my God prolong my breath
The saints may profit by't;
The saints, the glory of the earth,
The men of my delight.

3 Let heathens to their idols haste,
And worship wood or stone;
But my delightful lot is cast
Where the true God is known.

4 His hand provides my constant food,
He fills my daily cup;
Much am I pleas'd with present good,
But more rejoice in hope.

5 God is my portion and my joy,
His counsels are my light;
He gives me sweet advice by day,
And gentle hints by night.

6 My soul would all her thoughts approve
To his all-seeing eye;
Not death, nor hell my hope shall move,
While such a friend is nigh.

Psalm 16:5. Second Part. C. M.
The death and resurrection of Christ.

1 I Set the Lord before my face,
"He bears my courage up;

"My heart, and tongue, their joys express,
"My flesh shall rest in hope.

2 "My spirit, Lord, thou wilt not leave
"Where souls departed are;
"Nor quit my body to the grave
"To see corruption there.

3 "Thou wilt reveal the path of life,
"And raise me to thy throne;
"Thy courts immortal pleasure give,
"Thy presence joys unknown."

4 [Thus in the name of Christ, the Lord,
The holy David sung,
And Providence fulfils the word
Of his prophetic tongue.

5 Jesus, whom every saint adores,
Was crucify'd and slain;
Behold the tomb its prey restores,
Behold, he lives again!

6 When shall my feet arise and stand
On heaven's eternal hills?
There sits the Son at God's right hand,
And there the Father smiles.]

Psalm 17:1. 13 &c. S. M. Portion of saints and
sinners; or, Hope and despair in death.

1 Arise, my gracious God,
And make the wicked flee;
They are but thy chastising rod
To drive thy saints to thee.

2 Behold the sinner dies,
His haughty words are vain;
Here in this life his pleasure lies,
And all beyond is pain.

3 Then let his pride advance,
And boast of all his store:
The Lord is my inheritance,
My soul can wish no more.

4 I shall behold the face
Of my forgiving God,
And stand complete in righteousness,
Wash'd in my Saviour's blood.

5 There's a new heaven begun,
When I awake from death,
Drest in the likeness of thy Son,
And draw immortal breath.

Psalm 17:2. L. M. The sinner's portion, and
saint's hope; or, The heaven of separate souls,
and the resurrection.

1 Lord, I am thine; but thou wilt prove
My faith, my patience, and my love;
When men of spite against me join,
They are the sword, the hand is thine.

2 Their hope and portion lies below;
'Tis all the happiness they know,
'Tis all they seek; they take their shares,
And leave the rest among their heirs.

3 What sinners value, I resign;
Lord, 'tis enough that thou art mine;
I shall behold thy blissful face,
And stand complete in righteousness.

4 This life's a dream, an empty show;
But the bright world to which I go
Hath joys substantial and sincere;
When shall I wake, and find me there?

5 O glorious hour! O blest abode!
I shall be near and like my God!
And flesh and sin no more control
The sacred pleasures of the soul.

6 My flesh shall slumber in the ground,
Till the last trumpet's joyful sound;
Then burst the chains with sweet surprise,
And in my Saviour's image rise.

Psalm 18:1. 1-6 15-18. First Part. L. M.
Deliverance from despair; or, Temptations
overcome.

1 Thee will I love, O Lord, my strength,
My rock, my tower, my high defence,
Thy mighty arm shall be my trust,
For I have found salvation thence.

2 Death, and the terrors of the grave
Stood round me with their dismal shade;
While floods of high temptations rose,
And made my sinking soul afraid.

3 I saw the opening gates of hell,
With endless pains and sorrows there,
Which none but they that feel can tell,
While I was hurried to despair.

4 In my distress I call'd 'my God,'
When I could scarce believe him mine;
He bow'd his ear to my complaint,
Then did his grace appear divine.

5 [With speed he flew to my relief,
As on a cherub's wing he rode;
Awful and bright as lightning shone
The face of my deliverer, God.

6 Temptations fled at his rebuke,
The blast of his almighty breath;
He sent salvation from on high,
And drew me from the deeps of death.]

7 Great were my fears, my foes were great,
Much was their strength, and more their rage;
But Christ, my Lord, is conqueror still,
In all the wars that devils wage.

8 My song for ever shall record
That terrible, that joyful hour;
And give the glory to the Lord
Due to his mercy and his power.

Psalm 18:2. 20-26. Second Part. L. M.
Sincerity proved and rewarded.

1 Lord, thou hast seen my soul sincere,
Hast made thy truth and love appear;
Before mine eyes I set thy laws,
And thou hast own'd my righteous cause.

2 Since I have learnt thy holy ways,
I've walk'd upright before thy face;
Or if my feet did e'er depart,
'Twas never with a wicked heart.

3 What sore temptations broke my rest!
What wars and strugglings in my breast!

But thro' thy grace that reigns within,
I guard against my darling sin:

4 That sin which close besets me still,
That works and strives against my will;
When shall thy Spirit's sovereign power
Destroy it that it rise no more?

5 [With an impartial hand, the Lord
Deals out to mortals their reward;
The kind and faithful souls shall find
A God as faithful, and as kind.

6 The just and pure shall ever say,
Thou art more pure, more just than they;
And men that love revenge shall know,
God hath an arm of vengeance too.]

Psalm 18:3. 30 31 34 35 46. 3d Part. L. M.
Rejoicing in God; or, Salvation and triumph.

1 Just are thy ways, and true thy word,
Great rock of my secure abode;
Who is a God beside the Lord?
Or where's a refuge like our God?

2 'Tis he that girds me with his might,
Gives me his holy sword to wield;
And while with sin and hell I fight,
Spreads his salvation for my shield.

3 He lives (and blessed be my rock!)
The God of my salvation lives,
The dark designs of hell are broke;
Sweet is the peace my Father gives.

4 Before the scoffers of the age,
I will exalt my Father's name,
Nor tremble at their mighty rage,
But meet reproach and bear the shame.

5 To David and his royal seed
Thy grace for ever shall extend;
Thy love to saints in Christ their head
Knows not a limit, nor an end.

Psalm 18:4. First Part. C. M.
Victory and triumph over temporal enemies.

1 We love thee, Lord, and we adore,
Now is thine arm reveal'd;
Thou art our strength, our heavenly tower,
Our bulwark and our shield.

2 We fly to our eternal rock,
And find a sure defence;
His holy name our lips invoke,
And draw salvation thence.

3 When God, our leader, shines in arms,
What mortal heart can bear
The thunder of his loud alarms?
The lightning of his spear?

4 He rides upon the winged wind,
And angels in array
In millions wait to know his mind,
And swift as flames obey.

5 He speaks, and at his fierce rebuke,
Whole armies are dismay'd;
His voice, his frown, his angry look
Strikes all their courage dead.

6 He forms our generals for the field,
With all their dreadful skill;
Gives them his awful sword to wield,
And makes their hearts of steel.

7 [He arms our captains to the fight,
Tho' there his name's forgot:
He girded Cyrus with his might,
But Cyrus knew him not.

8 Oft has the Lord whole nations blest
For his own church's sake:
The powers that give his people rest,
Shall of his care partake.]

Psalm 18:5. Second Part. C. M.
The conqueror's song.

1 To thine almighty arm we owe
The triumphs of the day
Thy terrors, Lord, confound the foe,
And melt their strength away.

2 'Tis by thine aid our troops prevail,
And break united powers,

Or burn their boasted fleets, or scale
The proudest of their towers.

3 How have we chas'd them thro' the field,
And trod them to the ground,
While thy salvation was our shield,
But they no shelter found!

4 In vain to idol-saints they cry,
And perish in their blood;
Where is a rock so great, so high,
So powerful as our God?

5 The Rock of Israel ever lives,
His name be ever blest;
'Tis his own arm the victory gives,
And gives his people rest.

6 On kings that reign as David did,
He pours his blessings down;
Secures their honours to their seed,
And well supports the crown.

Psalm 19:1. First Part. S. M.
The book of nature and scripture.

For a Lord's-day morning.

1 Behold the lofty sky
Declares its maker God,
And all his starry works on high
Proclaim his power abroad.

2 The darkness and the light
Still keep their course the same;
While night to day, and day to night
Divinely teach his name.

3 In every different land
Their general voice is known
They shew the wonders of his hand,
And orders of his throne.

4 Ye British lands, rejoice,
Here he reveals his word,
We are not left to nature's voice
To bid us know the Lord.

5 His statutes and commands
Are set before our eyes;
He puts his gospel in our hands,
Where our salvation lies.

6 His laws are just and pure,
His truth without deceit,
His promises for ever sure,
And his rewards are great.

7 [Not honey to the taste
Affords so much delight,
Nor gold that has the furnace past
So much allures the sight.

8 While of thy works I sing,
Thy glory to proclaim,
Accept the praise, my God, my King,
In my Redeemer's name.]

Psalm 19:2. Second Part. S. M.
God's word most excellent; or,
Sincerity and watchfulness.

For a Lord's-day morning.

1 Behold the morning sun
Begins his glorious way;
His beams thro' all the nations run,
And life and light convey.

2 But where the gospel comes,
It spreads diviner light,
It calls dead sinners from their tombs,
And gives the blind their sight.

3 How perfect is thy word!
And all thy judgments just!
For ever sure thy promise, Lord,
And men securely trust.

4 My gracious God, how plain
Are thy directions given!
O! may I never read in vain,
But find the path to heaven!

PAUSE.

5 I hear thy word with love,
And I would fain obey;

Send thy good Spirit from above
To guide me, lest I stray.

6 O who can ever find
The errors of his ways?
Yet, with a bold presumptuous mind,
I would not dare transgress.

7 Warn me of every sin,
Forgive my secret faults,
And cleanse this guilty soul of mine,
Whose crimes exceed my thoughts.

8 While with my heart and tongue
I spread thy praise abroad,
Accept the worship and the song,
My Saviour and my God.

Psalm 19:3. L. M. The books of nature and of
scripture compared; or, The glory and success
of the gospel.

1 The heavens declare thy glory, Lord,
In every star thy wisdom shines;
But when our eyes behold thy word
We read thy name in fairer lines.

2 The rolling sun, the changing light,
And nights and days thy power confess;
But the blest volume thou hast writ
Reveals thy justice and thy grace.

3 Sun, moon, and stars convey thy praise
Round the whole earth, and never stand;
So when thy truth begun its race,
It touch'd and glanc'd on every land.

4 Nor shall thy spreading gospel rest,
Till thro' the world thy truth has run;
Till Christ has all the nations blest,
That see the light, or feel the sun.

5 Great Sun of Righteousness, arise,
Bless the dark world with heavenly light;
Thy gospel makes the simple wise,
Thy laws are pure, thy judgments right.

6 Thy noblest wonders here we view
In souls renew'd and sins forgiven:

Lord, cleanse my sins, my soul renew,
And make thy word my guide to heaven.

Psalm 19:4.
To the tune of the 113th Psalm.
The book of nature and scripture.

1 Great God, the heaven's well-order'd frame
Declares the glories of thy name;
There thy rich works of wonder shine:
A thousand starry beauties there,
A thousand radiant marks appear
Of boundless power and skill divine.

2 From night to day, from day to night,
The dawning and the dying light
Lectures of heavenly wisdom read;
With silent eloquence they raise
Our thoughts to our Creator's praise,
And neither sound nor language need.

3 Yet their divine instructions run
Far as the journies of the sun,
And every nation knows their voice;
The sun, like some young bridegroom drest,
Breaks from the chambers of the east,
Rolls round, and makes the earth rejoice.

4 Where'er he spreads his beams abroad,
He smiles and speaks his maker God;
All nature joins to shew thy praise:
Thus God, in every creature shines;
Fair is the book of nature's lines,
But fairer is thy book of grace.

PAUSE.

5 I love the volumes of thy word;
What light and joy those leaves afford
To souls benighted and distrest!
Thy precepts guide my doubtful way,
Thy fear forbids my feet to stray;
Thy promise leads my heart to rest.

6 From the discoveries of thy law
The perfect rules of life I draw,
These are my study and delight:
Not honey so invites the taste,
Nor gold, that hath the furnace past,
Appears so pleasing to the sight.

7 Thy threatenings wake my slumbering eyes,
And warn me where my danger lies;
But 'tis thy blessed gospel, Lord,
That makes my guilty conscience clean,
Converts my soul, subdues my sin,
And gives a free but large reward.

8 Who knows the errors of his thoughts?
My God, forgive my secret faults,
And from presumptuous sins restrain;
Accept my poor attempts of praise
That I have read thy book of grace,
And book of nature, not in vain.

Psalm 20.
Prayer and hope of victory.
For a day of prayer in time of war.

1 Now may the God of power and grace
Attend his people's humble cry!
Jehovah hears when Israel prays,
And brings deliverance from on high.

2 The name of Jacob's God defends
Better than shields or brazen walls;
He from his sanctuary sends
Succour and strength, when Zion calls.

3 Well he remembers all our sighs,
His love exceeds our best deserts,
His love accepts the sacrifice
Of humble groans and broken hearts.

4 In his salvation is our hope,
And, in the name of Israel's God,
Our troops shall lift their banners up,
Our navies spread their flags abroad.

5 Some trust in horses train'd for war,
And some of chariots make their boast;
Our surest expectations are
From thee, the Lord of heavenly hosts.

6 [O! may the memory of thy name
Inspire our armies for the fight!
Our foes shall fall and die with shame,
Or quit the field with shameful flight.]

7 Now save us, Lord, from slavish fear;
Now let our hopes be firm and strong,
Till the salvation shall appear,
And joy and triumph raise the song.

Psalm 21:1. C. M.
Our king is the care of heaven.

1 The king, O Lord, with songs of praise,
Shall in thy strength rejoice;
And, blest with thy salvation, raise
To heaven his cheerful voice.

2 Thy sure defence, thro' nations round,
Has spread his glorious name;
And his successful actions crown'd
With majesty and fame.

3 Then let the king on God alone
For timely aid rely;
His mercy shall support the throne,
And all our wants supply.

4 But, righteous Lord, his stubborn foes
Shall feel thy dreadful hand
Thy vengeful arm shall find out those
That hate his mild command.

5 When thou against them dost engage,
Thy just but dreadful doom
Shall, like a fiery oven's rage,
Their hopes and them consume.

6 Thus, Lord, thy wondrous power declare,
And thus exalt thy fame;
Whilst we glad songs of praise prepare
For thine almighty name.

Psalm 21:2. 1-9. L. M.
Christ exalted to the kingdom.

1 David rejoic'd in God his strength,
Rais'd to the throne by special grace;
But Christ, the Son, appears at length,
Fulfils the triumph and the praise.

2 How great is the Messiah's joy
In the salvation of thy hand!
Lord, thou hast rais'd his kingdom high,
And given the world to his command.

3 Thy goodness grants whate'er he will,
Nor doth the least request withhold;
Blessings of love prevent him still,
And crowns of glory, not of gold.

4 Honour and majesty divine
Around his sacred temples shine;
Blest with the favour of thy face,
And length of everlasting days.

5 Thy hand shall find out all his foes;
And as a fiery oven glows
With raging heat and living coals,
So shall thy wrath devour their souls.

Psalm 22:1. 1-16. First Part. C. M,
The sufferings and death of Christ.

1 "Why has my God my soul forsook,
"Nor will a smile afford?"
(Thus David once in anguish spoke,
And thus our dying Lord.)

2 Tho' 'tis thy chief delight to dwell
Among thy praising saints,
Yet thou canst hear a groan as well,
And pity our complaints.

3 Our fathers trusted in thy name,
And great deliverance found;
But I'm a worm, despis'd of men,
And trodden to the ground.

4 Shaking the head they pass me by,
And laugh my soul to scorn;
"In vain he trusts in God" they cry,
"Neglected and forlorn."

5 But thou art he who form'd my flesh
By thine almighty word,
And since I hung upon the breast,
My hope is in the Lord.

6 Why will my Father hide his face,
When foes stand threatening round,
In the dark hour of deep distress,
And not an helper found?

PAUSE.

7 Behold thy darling left among
The cruel and the proud,
As bulls of Bashan fierce and strong,
As lions roaring loud.

8 From earth and hell my sorrows meet
To multiply the smart;
They nail my hands, they pierce my feet
And try to vex my heart.

9 Yet if thy sovereign hand let loose
The rage of earth and hell,
Why will my heavenly Father bruise
The Son he loves so well?

10 My God, if possible it be,
Withhold this bitter cup;
But I resign my will to thee,
And drink the sorrows up.

11 My heart dissolves with pangs unknown
In groans I waste my breath;
Thy heavy hand has brought me down
Low as the dust of death.

12 Father, I give my spirit up;
And trust it in thy hand;
My dying flesh shall rest in hope,
And rise at thy command.

Psalm 22:2. 20 21 27-31. 2d Part. C. M.
Christ's sufferings and kingdom.

1 "Now from the roaring lion's rage,
"O Lord, protect thy Son;
"Nor leave thy darling to engage,
"The powers of hell alone."

2 Thus did our suffering Saviour pray,
With mighty cries and tears;
God heard him in that dreadful day,
And chas'd away his fears.

3 Great was the victory of his death,
His throne exalted high;
And all the kindreds of the earth
Shall worship or shall die.

4 A numerous offspring must arise
From his expiring groans;

They shall be reckon'd in his eyes
For daughters and for sons.

5 The meek and humble soul shall see
His table richly spread;
And all that seek the Lord shall be
With joys immortal fed.

6 The isles shall know the righteousness
Of our incarnate God;
And nations yet unborn profess
Salvation in his blood.

Psalm 22:3. L. M.
Christ's sufferings and exaltation.

1 Now let our mournful songs record
The dying sorrows of our Lord;
When he complain'd in tears and blood
As one forsaken of his God.

2 The Jews beheld him thus forlorn,
And shake their heads, and laugh in scorn;
"He rescu'd others from the grave,
"Now let him try himself to save.

3 "This is the man did once pretend
"God was his father and his friend;
"If God the blessed lov'd him so,
"Why doth he fail to help him now?"

4 Barbarous people! cruel priests!
How they stood round like savage beasts!
Like lions gaping to devour,
When God had left him in their power.

5 They wound his head, his hands, his feet,
Till streams of blood each other meet;
By lot his garments they divide
And mock the pangs in which he dy'd.

6 But God, his Father, heard his cry:
Rais'd from the dead he reigns on high.
The nations learn his righteousness,
And humble sinners taste his grace.

Psalm 23:1. L. M.
God our Shepherd.

1 My shepherd is the living Lord;
Now shall my wants be well supply'd
His providence and holy word
Become my safety and my guide.

2 In pastures where salvation grows
He makes me feed, he makes me rest;
There living water gently flows,
And all the food's divinely blest.

3 My wandering feet his ways mistake,
But he restores my soul to peace,
And leads me for his mercy's sake,
In the fair paths of righteousness.

4 Tho' I walk thro' the gloomy vale,
Where death and all its terrors are,
My heart and hope shall never fail,
For God my shepherd's with me there.

5 Amidst the darkness and the deeps
Thou art my comfort, thou my stay;
Thy staff supports my feeble steps,
Thy rod directs my doubtful way.

6 The sons of earth and sons of hell
Gaze at thy goodness and repine
To see my table spread so well
With living bread and cheerful wine.

7 [How I rejoice when on my head
Thy Spirit condescends to rest!
'Tis a divine anointing shed
Like oil of gladness at a feast.

8 Surely the mercies of the Lord
Attend his household all their days;
There will I dwell to hear his word,
To seek his face, and sing his praise.]

Psalm 23:2. C. M.
The same.

1. My Shepherd will supply my need,
Jehovah is his name;
In pastures fresh he makes me feed
Beside the living stream.

2 He brings my wandering spirit back,
When I forsake his ways;

And leads me for his mercy's sake,
In paths of truth and grace.

3 When I walk thro' the shades of death,
Thy presence is my stay;
A word of thy supporting breath
Drives all my fears away.

4 Thy hand, in spite of all my foes,
Doth still my table spread;
My cup with blessings overflows,
Thine oil anoints my head.

5 The sure provisions of my God
Attend me all my days;
O may thy house be mine abode,
And all my work be praise!

6 There would I find a settled rest,
(While others go and come)
No more a stranger or a guest,
But like a child at home.

Psalm 23:3. S. M.
The same.

1 The Lord my shepherd is,
I shall be well supply'd;
Since he is mine, and I am his,
What can I want beside?

2 He leads me to the place
Where heavenly pasture grows,
Where living waters gently pass,
And full salvation flows.

3 If e'er I go astray,
He doth my soul reclaim,
And guides me in his own right way,
For his most holy name.

4 While he affords his aid,
I cannot yield to fear;
Tho' I should walk thro' death's dark shade
My Shepherd's with me there.

5 In spite of all my foes,
Thou dost my table spread,
My cup with blessings overflows,
And joy exalts my head.

6 The bounties of thy love
Shall crown my following days;
Nor from thy house will I remove,
Nor cease to speak thy praise.

Psalm 24:1. C. M.
Dwelling with God.

1 The earth for ever is the Lord's,
With Adam's numerous race;
He rais'd its arches o'er the floods,
And built it on the seas.

2 But who among the sons of men
May visit thine abode?
He that has hands from mischief clean,
Whose heart is right with God.

3 This is the man may rise, and take
The blessings of his grace;
This is the lot of those that seek
The God of Jacob's face.

4 Now let our soul's immortal powers
To meet the Lord prepare,
Lift up their everlasting doors,
The King of glory's near.

5 The King of glory! who can tell
The wonders of his might!
He rules the nations; but to dwell
With saints is his delight.

Psalm 24:2. L. M.
Saints dwell in heaven; or, Christ's ascension.

1 This spacious earth is all the Lord's,
And men, and worms, and beasts, and birds:
He rais'd the building on the seas,
And gave it for their dwelling-place.

2 But there's a brighter world on high,
Thy palace, Lord, above the sky:
Who shall ascend that blest abode,
And dwell so near his Maker God?

3 He that abhors and fears to sin,
Whose heart is pure whose hands are clean,

Him shall the Lord the Saviour bless,
And clothe his soul with righteousness.

4 These are the men, the pious race
That seek the God of Jacob's face;
These shall enjoy the blissful sight,
And dwell in everlasting light.

PAUSE.

5 Rejoice, ye shining worlds on high,
Behold the King of glory nigh!
Who can this King of glory be?
The mighty Lord, the Saviour's he.

6 Ye heavenly gates, your leaves display
To make the Lord the Saviour way:
Laden with spoils from earth and hell,
The conqueror comes with God to dwell.

7 Rais'd from the dead he goes before,
He opens heaven's eternal door,
To give his saints a blest abode
Near their Redeemer, and their God.

Psalm 25:1. 1-11. First Part.
Waiting for pardon and direction.

1 I Lift my soul to God,
My trust is in his name;
Let not my foes that seek my blood
Still triumph in my shame.

2 Sin and the powers of hell
Persuade me to despair;
Lord, make me know thy covenant well,
That I may 'scape the snare.

3 From the first dawning light
Till the dark evening rise,
For thy salvation, Lord, I wait
With ever-longing eyes.

4 Remember all thy grace,
And lead me in thy truth;
Forgive the sins of riper days,
And follies of my youth.

5 The Lord is just and kind,
The meek shall learn his ways;

And every humble sinner find
The methods of his grace.

6 For his own goodness' sake
He saves my soul from shame;
He pardons (tho' my guilt be great)
Thro' my Redeemer's name.

Psalm 25:2. 12 14 10 13. Second Part.
Divine instruction.

1 Where shall the man be found
That fears t' offend his God,
That loves the gospel's joyful sound,
And trembles at the rod?

2 The Lord shall make him know
The secrets of his heart,
The wonders of his covenant show,
And all his love impart.

3 The dealings of his hand
Are truth and mercy still
With such as to his covenant stand,
And love to do his will.

4 Their souls shall dwell at ease
Before their Maker's face,
Their seed shall taste the promises,
In their extensive grace.

Psalm 25:3. 15-22. Third Part.
Distress of soul; or, Backsliding and desertion.

1 Mine eyes and my desire
Are ever to the Lord;
I love to plead his promises,
And rest upon his word.

2 Turn, turn thee to my soul,
Bring thy salvation near:
When will thy hand release my feet
Out of the deadly snare?

3 When shall the sovereign grace
Of my forgiving God
Restore me from those dangerous ways
My wandering feet have trod?

4 The tumult of my thoughts
Doth but enlarge my woe;
My spirit languishes, my heart
Is desolate and low.

5 With every morning light
My sorrow new begins;
Look on my anguish and my pain,
And pardon all my sins.

PAUSE.

6 Behold the hosts of hell
How cruel is their hate!
Against my life they rise, and join
Their fury with deceit.

7 O keep my soul from death,
Nor put my hope to shame,
For I have plac'd my only trust
In my Redeemer's name.

8 With humble faith I wait
To see thy face again;
Of Israel it shall ne'er be said,
"He sought the Lord in vain."

Psalm 26.
Self-examination; or, Evidences of grace.

1 Judge me, O Lord, and prove my ways,
And try my reins, and try my heart;
My faith upon thy promise stays,
Nor from thy law my feet depart.

2 I hate to walk, I hate to sit,
With men of vanity and lies;
The scoffer and the hypocrite
Are the abhorrence of mine eyes.

3 Amongst thy saints will I appear,
With hands well wash'd in innocence;
But when I stand before thy bar,
The blood of Christ is my defence.

4 I love thy habitation, Lord,
The temple where thine honours dwell;
There shall I hear thine holy word,
And there thy works of wonder tell.

5 Let not my soul be join'd at last
With men of treachery and blood,
Since I my days on earth have past
Among the saints, and near my God.

Psalm 27:1. 1-6. First Part.
The church is our delight and safety.

1 The Lord of glory is my light,
And my salvation too;
God is my strength, nor will I fear
What all my foes can do.

2 One privilege my heart desires;
O grant me an abode
Among the churches of thy saints,
The temples of my God!

3 There shall I offer my requests,
And see thy beauty still,
Shall hear thy messages of love,
And there enquire thy will.

4 When troubles rise, and storms appear,
There may his children hide:
God has a strong pavilion where
He makes my soul abide.

5 Now shall my head be lifted high
Above my foes around,
And songs of joy and victory
Within thy temple sound.

Psalm 27:2. 8 9 13 14. Second Part.

Prayer and Hope.

1 Soon as I heard my Father say,
"Ye children, seek my grace;"
My heart reply'd without delay,
"I'll seek my Father's face."

2 Let not thy face be hid from me,
Nor frown my soul away;
God of my life, I fly to thee
In a distressing day.

3 Should friends and kindred near and dear
Leave me to want, or die,

My God would make my life his care
And all my need supply.

4 My fainting flesh had dy'd with grief,
Had not my soul believ'd
To see thy grace provide relief,
Nor was my hope deceiv'd.

5 Wait on the Lord, ye trembling saints,
And keep your courage up;
He'll raise your spirit when it faints,
And far exceed your hope.

Psalm 29. L. M.
Storm and thunder.

1 Give to the Lord, ye sons of fame,
Give to the Lord renown and power,
Ascribe due honours to his name,
And his eternal might adore.

2 The Lord proclaims his power aloud
Over the ocean and the land;
His voice divides the watery cloud,
And lightnings blaze at his command.

3 He speaks, and tempest, hail, and wind,
Lay the wide forests bare around;
The fearful hart, and frighted hind,
Leap at the terror of the sound.

4 To Lebanon he turns his voice,
And, lo, the stately cedars break;
The mountains tremble at the noise,
The vallies roar, the deserts quake.

5 The Lord sits sovereign on the flood,
The thunderer reigns for ever king;
But makes his church his blest abode,
Where we his awful glories sing.

6 In gentler language there the Lord
The counsels of his grace imparts;
Amidst the raging storm his word
Speaks peace and courage to our hearts.

Psalm 30:1. First Part.
Sickness healed, and sorrow removed.

1 I will extol thee, Lord, on high,
At thy command, diseases fly;
Who but a God can speak and save
From the dark borders of the grave?

2 Sing to the Lord, ye saints of his,
And tell how large his goodness is;
Let all your powers rejoice and bless,
While you record his holiness.

3 His anger but a moment stays
His love is life and length of days;
Tho' grief and tears the night employ,
The morning-star restores the joy.

Psalm 30:2. 6. Second Part.
Health, sickness, and recovery.

1 Firm was my health, my day was bright,
And I presum'd 'twould ne'er be night;
Fondly I said within my heart,
"Pleasure and peace shall ne'er depart."

2 But I forgot thine arm was strong,
Which made my mountain stand so long;
Soon as thy face began to hide,
My health was gone, my comforts dy'd.

3 I cry'd aloud to thee, my God,
"What canst thou profit by my blood?
"Deep in the dust can I declare
"Thy truth, or sing thy goodness there?

4 "Hear me, O God of grace," I said,
"And bring me from among the dead:"
Thy word rebuk'd the pains I felt,
Thy pardoning love remov'd my guilt.

5 My groans, and tears, and forms of woe,
Are turn'd to joy and praises now;
I throw my sackcloth on the ground,
And ease and gladness gird me round.

6 My tongue, the glory of my frame,
Shall ne'er be silent of thy name
Thy praise shall sound thro' earth and heaven,
For sickness heal'd, and sins forgiven.

Psalm 31:1. 5 13-19 22 23. First Part.
Deliverance from death.

1 Into thine hand, 0 God of truth,
My spirit I commit;
Thou hast redeem'd my soul from death,
And sav'd me from the pit.

2 The passions of my hope and fear
Maintain'd a doubtful strife,
While sorrow, pain, and sin conspir'd
To take away my life.

3 "My times are in thine hand," I cry'd,
"Tho' I draw near the dust ;"
Thou art the refuge where I hide,
The God in whom I trust.

4 O make thy reconciled face
Upon thy servant shine,
And save me for thy mercy's sake,
For I'm entirely thine.

PAUSE.

5 ['Twas in my haste, my spirit said,
"I must despair and die,
"I am cut off before thine eyes;"
But thou hast heard me cry.]

6 Thy goodness how divinely free!
How wondrous is thy grace
To those that fear thy majesty,
And trust thy promises!

7 O love the Lord, all ye his saints,
And sing his praises loud;
He'll bend his ear to your complaints,
And recompense the proud.

Psalm 31:2. 7-13 18-21. Second Part.
Deliverance from slander and reproach.

1 My heart rejoices in thy name,
My God, my help, my trust;
Thou hast preserv'd my face from shame,
Mine honour from the dust.

2 "My life is spent with grief," I cry'd,
"My years consum'd in groans,

"My strength decays, mine eyes are dry'd,
"And sorrow wastes my bones."

3 Among mine enemies my name
Was a mere proverb grown,
While to my neighbours I became
Forgotten and unknown.

4 Slander and fear on every side,
Seiz'd and beset me round;
I to the throne of grace apply'd,
And speedy rescue found.

PAUSE.

5 How great deliverance thou hast wrought
Before the sons of men!
The lying lips to silence brought,
And made their boastings vain!

6 Thy children, from the strife of tongues,
Shall thy pavilion hide,
Guard them from infamy and wrongs,
And crush the sons of pride.

7 Within thy secret presence, Lord,
Let me for ever dwell;
No fenced city, wall'd and barr'd,
Secures a saint so well.

Psalm 32:1. S. M.
Forgiveness of sins upon confession.

1 O blessed souls are they Whose sins are
cover'd o'er! Divinely blest, to whom the Lord
imputes their guilt no more.

2 They mourn their follies past,
And keep their hearts with care;
Their lips and lives without deceit,
Shall prove their faith sincere.

3 While I conceal'd my guilt
I felt the festering wound,
Till I confess'd my sins to thee,
And ready pardon found.

4 Let sinners learn to pray,
Let saints keep near the throne;

Our help in times of deep distress,
Is found in God alone.

Psalm 32:2. First Part. L. M. Free pardon and
sincere obedience; or, Confession and
forgiveness.

1 Happy the man to whom his God
No more imputes his sin,
But wash'd in the Redeemer's blood,
Hath made his garments clean!

2 Happy, beyond expression, he
Whose debts are thus discharg'd;
And from the guilty bondage free,
He feels his soul enlarg'd.

3 His spirit hates deceit and lies,
His words are all sincere;
He guards his heart, he guards his eyes,
To keep his conscience clear.

4 While I my inward guilt supprest,
No quiet could I find;
Thy wrath lay burning in my breast,
And rack'd my tortur'd mind.

5 Then I confess'd my troubled thoughts,
My secret sins reveal'd;
Thy pardoning grace forgave my faults,
Thy grace my pardon seal'd.

6 This shall invite thy saints to pray,
When, like a raging flood,
Temptations rise, our strength and stay
Is a forgiving God.

Psalm 32:3. L. M. Repentance and free pardon;
or, Justification and sanctification.

1 Blest is the man, for ever blest,
Whose guilt is pardon'd by his God,
Whose sins with sorrow are confess'd,
And cover'd with his Saviour's blood.

2 Blest is the man to whom the Lord
Imputes not his iniquities,
He pleads no merit of reward,
And not on works, but grace relies.

3 From guile his heart and lips are free,
His humble joy, his holy fear,
With deep repentance well agree,
And join to prove his faith sincere.

4 How glorious is that righteousness
That hides and cancels all his sins!
While a bright evidence of grace
Thro' his whole life appears and shines.

Psalm 32:4. Second Part. L. M.
A guilty conscience eased by confession and
pardon.

1 While I keep silence, and conceal
My heavy guilt within my heart,
What torments doth my conscience feel!
What agonies of inward smart!

2 I spread my sins before the Lord,
And all my secret faults confess;
Thy gospel speaks a pard'ning word
Thine Holy Spirit seals the grace.

3 For this shall every humble soul
Make swift addresses to thy seat;
When floods of huge temptations roll,
There shall they find a blest retreat.

4 How safe beneath thy wings I lie,
When days grow dark, and storms appear!
And when I walk, thy watchful eye
Shall guide me safe from every snare.

Psalm 33:1. First Part. C. M.
Works of creation and providence.

1 Rejoice, ye righteous, in the Lord,
This work belongs to you:
Sing of his name, his ways, his word,
How holy, just, and true!

2 His mercy and his righteousness
Let heaven and earth proclaim;
His works of nature and of grace
Reveal his wondrous name.

3 His wisdom and almighty word
The heavenly arches spread;

And by the Spirit of the Lord
Their shining hosts were made.

4 He bid the liquid waters flow
To their appointed deep;
The flowing seas their limits know,
And their own station keep.

5 Ye tenants of the spacious earth,
With fear before him stand;
He spake, and nature took its birth,
And rests on his command.

6 He scorns the angry nations' rage,
And breaks their vain designs;
His counsel stands thro' every age,
And in full glory shines.

Psalm 33:2. Second Part. C. M.
Creatures vain, and God all-sufficient.

1 Blest is the nation where the Lord
Hath fix'd his gracious throne;
Where he reveals his heavenly word,
And calls their tribes his own.

2 His eye, with infinite survey,
Does the whole world behold;
He form'd us all of equal clay,
And knows our feeble mould.

3 Kings are not rescu'd by the force
Of armies from the grave;
Nor speed nor courage of an horse
Can the bold rider save,

4 Vain is the strength of beasts or men
To hope for safety thence;
But holy souls from God obtain
A strong and sure defence.

5 God is their fear, and God their trust,
When plagues or famine spread,
His watchful eye secures the just
Amongst ten thousand dead.

6 Lord, let our hearts in thee rejoice,
And bless us from thy throne;
For we have made thy word our choice,
And trust thy grace alone.

Psalm 33:3. First Part. As the 113th Psalm.
Works of creation and providence.

1 Ye holy souls, in God rejoice,
Your Maker's praise becomes your voice;
Great is your theme, your songs be new:
Sing of his name, his word, his ways,
His works of nature and of grace,
How wise and holy, just and true.

2 Justice and truth he ever loves,
And the whole earth his goodness proves,
His word the heavenly arches spread;
How wide they shine from north to south!
And by the Spirit of his mouth
Were all the starry armies made.

3 He gathers the wide-flowing seas,
Those watery treasures know their place,
In the vast storehouse of the deep:
He spake, and gave all nature birth;
And fires, and seas, and heaven, and earth,
His everlasting orders keep.

4 Let mortals tremble and adore
A God of such resistless power,
Nor dare indulge their feeble rage:
Vain are your thoughts, and weak your hands;
But his eternal counsel stands,
And rules the world from age to age.

Psalm 33:4. Second Part. As the 113th Psalm.
Creatures vain, and God all-sufficient.

1 O Happy nation, where the Lord
Reveals the treasure of his word,
And builds his church his earthly throne!
His eye the heathen world surveys,
He form'd their hearts, he knows their ways;
But God their Maker is unknown.

2 Let kings rely upon their host,
And of his strength the champion boast;
In vain they boast, in vain rely;
In vain we trust the brutal force,
Or speed, or courage of an horse,
To guard his rider, or to fly.

3 The eye of thy compassion, Lord,
Doth more secure defence afford

When death or dangers threatening stand;
Thy watchful eye preserves the just,
Who make thy name their fear and trust,
When wars or famine waste the land.

4 In sickness or the bloody field,
Thou our physician, thou our shield,
Send us salvation from thy throne;
We wait to see thy goodness shine;
Let us rejoice in help divine,
For all our hope is God alone.

Psalm 34:1. First Part. L. M.
God's care of the saints; or, Deliverance by
prayer.

1 Lord, I will bless thee all my days,
Thy praise shall dwell upon my tongue;
My soul shall glory in thy grace,
While saints rejoice to hear the song.

2 Come, magnify the Lord with me,
Come, let us all exalt his name;
I sought th' eternal God, and he
Has not expos'd my hope to shame.

3 I told him all my secret grief,
My secret groaning reach'd his ears;
He gave my inward pains relief,
And calm'd the tumult of my fears.

4 To him the poor lift up their eyes,
Their faces feel the heavenly shine;
A beam of mercy from the skies
Fills them with light and joy divine.

6 His holy angels pitch their tents
Around the men that serve the Lord;
O fear and love him, all his saints,
Taste of his grace and trust his word.

6 The wild young lions, pinch'd with pain
And hunger, roar thro' all the wood;
But none shall seek the Lord in vain,
Nor want supplies of real good.

Psalm 34:2. 11-22. Second Part. L. M.
Religious education; or, Instructions of piety.

1 Children in years and knowledge young,
Your parents' hope, your parents' joy,
Attend the counsels of my tongue,
Let pious thoughts your minds employ.

2 If you desire a length of days,
And peace to crown your mortal state,
Restrain your feet from impious ways,
Your lips from slander and deceit.

3 The eyes of God regard his saints,
His ears are open to their cries;
He sets his frowning face against
The sons of violence and lies.

4 To humble souls and broken hearts
God with his grace is ever nigh;
Pardon and hope his love imparts
When men in deep contrition lie.

5 He tell their tears, he counts their groans,
His Son redeems their souls from death;
His Spirit heals their broken bones,
They in his praise employ their breath.

Psalm 34:3. 1-10. First Part. C. M.
Prayer and Praise for eminent deliverance.

1 I'll bless the Lord from day to day;
How good are all his ways!
Ye humble souls that use to pray,
Come, help my lips to praise.

2 Sing to the honour of his name,
How a poor sufferer cry'd,
Nor was his hope expos'd to shame,
Nor was his suit deny'd.

3 When threatening sorrows round me stood,
And endless fears arose,
Like the loud billows of a flood,
Redoubling all my woes;

4 I told the Lord my sore distress
With heavy groans and tears,
He gave my sharpest torments ease,
And silenc'd all my fears.

PAUSE.

5 [O sinners, come and taste his love,
Come, learn his pleasant ways,
And let your own experience prove
The sweetness of his grace.

6 He bids his angels pitch their tents
Round where his children dwell
What ills their heavenly care prevents
No earthly tongue can tell.]

7 [O love the Lord, ye saints of his;
His eye regards the just;
How richly blest their portion is
Who make the Lord their trust!

8 Young lions pinch'd with hunger roar,
And famish in the wood;
But God supplies his holy poor
With every needful good.]

Psalm 34:4. 11-22. Second Part. C. M.
Exhortations to peace and Holiness.

1 Come, children, learn to fear the Lord;
And that your days be long,
Let not a false or spiteful word
Be found upon your tongue.

2 Depart from mischief, practise love,
Pursue the works of peace;
So shall the Lord your ways approve,
And set your souls at ease.

3 His eyes awake to guard the just,
His ears attend their cry;
When broken spirits dwell in dust,
The God of grace is nigh.

4 What tho' the sorrows here they taste
Are sharp and tedious too,
The Lord, who saves them all at last,
Is their supporter now.

5 Evil shall smite the wicked dead;
But God secures his own,
Prevents the mischief when they slide,
Or heals the broken bone.

6 When desolation like a flood,
O'er the proud sinner rolls,

Saints find a refuge in their God,
For he redeem'd their souls.

Psalm 35:1. 1-9. First Part. Prayer and faith of
persecuted saints; or, Imprecations mixed with
charity.

1 Now plead my cause, almighty God,
With all the Sons of strife;
And fight against the men of blood,
Who fight against my life.

2 Draw out thy spear and stop their way,
Lift thine avenging rod;
But to my soul in mercy say,
"I am thy Saviour God."

3 They plant their snares to catch my feet,
And nets of mischief spread;
Plunge the destroyers in the pit
That their own hands have made.

4 Let fogs and darkness hide their way,
And slippery be their ground;
Thy wrath shall make their lives a prey,
And all their rage confound.

5 They fly like chaff before the wind,
Before thine angry breath;
The angel of the Lord behind
Pursues them down to death.

6 They love the road that leads to hell;
Then let the rebels die
Whose malice is implacable
Against the Lord on high.

7 But if thou hast a chosen few
Amongst that impious race,
Divide them from the bloody crew
By thy surprising grace.

8 Then will I raise my tuneful voice
To make thy wonders known;
In their salvation I'll rejoice,
And bless thee for my own.

Psalm 35:2. 12-14. Second Part.
Love to enemies; or, The love of
Christ to sinners typified in David.

1 Behold the love, the generous love
That holy David shows;
Hark, how his sounding bowels move
To his afflicted foes!

2 When they are sick his soul complains,
And seems to feel the smart;
The spirit of the gospel reigns,
And melts his pious heart.

3 How did his flowing tears condole
As for a brother dead!
And fasting mortify'd his soul,
While for their life he pray'd.

4 They groan'd; and curs'd him on their bed,
Yet still he pleads and mourns;
And double blessings on his head
The righteous God returns.

5 O glorious type of heavenly grace!
Thus Christ the Lord appears;
While sinners curse, the Saviour prays,
And pities them with tears.

6 He, the true David, Israel's king,
Blest and belov'd of God,
To save us rebels dead in sin,
Paid his own dearest blood.

Psalm 36:1. 5-9. L. M. The perfections and
providence of God; or, General providence and
special grace.

1 High in the heavens, eternal God,
Thy goodness in full glory shines;
Thy truth shall break thro' every cloud
That veils and darkens thy designs.

2 For ever firm thy justice stands,
As mountains their foundations keep;
Wise are the wonders of thy hands;
Thy judgments are a mighty deep.

3 Thy providence is kind and large,
Both man and beast thy bounty share;

The whole creation is thy charge,
But saints are thy peculiar care.

4 My God! how excellent thy grace,
Whence all our hope and comfort springs!
The sons of Adam in distress
Fly to the shadow of thy wings.

5 From the provisions of thy house
We shall be fed with sweet repast;
There mercy like a river flows,
And brings salvation to our taste.

6 Life, like a fountain rich and free
Springs from the presence of the Lord;
And in thy light our souls shall see
The glories promis'd in thy word.

Psalm 36:2. 1 2 5 6 7 9 C. M.
Practical atheism exposed; or,
The being and attributes of God asserted.

1 While men grow bold in wicked ways!
And yet a God they own,
My heart within me often says,
"Their thoughts believe there's none."

2 Their thoughts and ways at once declare
(Whate'er their lips profess)
God hath no wrath for them to fear,
Nor will they seek his grace.

3 What strange self-flattery blinds their eyes!
But there's an hastening hour
When they shall see with sore surprise
The terrors of thy power.

4 Thy justice shall maintain its throne,
Tho' mountains melt away;
Thy judgments are a world unknown,
A deep unfathom'd sea.

5 Above the heavens' created rounds,
Thy mercies, Lord, extend;
Thy truth outlives the narrow bounds,
Where time and nature end.

6 Safety to man thy goodness brings,
Nor overlooks the beast;

Beneath the shadow of thy wings
Thy children choose to rest.

7 [From thee, when creature-streams run low,
And mortal comforts die,
Perpetual springs of life shall flow,
And raise our pleasures high.

8 Tho' all created light decay,
And death close up our eyes
Thy presence makes eternal day
Where clouds can never rise.]

Psalm 36:3. 1-7. S. M. The wickedness of man,
and the majesty of God; or. Practical atheism
exposed.

1 When man grows bold in sin
My heart within me cries,
"He hath no faith of God within,
Nor fear before his eyes."

2 [He walks awhile conceal'd
In a self-flattering dream,
Till his dark crimes at once reveal'd
Expose his hateful name.]

3 His heart is false and foul,
His words are smooth and fair;
Wisdom is banish'd from his soul,
And leaves no goodness there.

4 He plots upon his bed
New mischiefs to fulfil;
He sets his heart, and hand, and head,
To practise all that's ill.

5 But there's a dreadful God,
Tho' men renounce his fear;
His justice hid behind the cloud
Shall one great day appear.

6 His truth transcends the sky;
In heaven his mercies dwell;
Deep as the sea his judgments lie,
His anger burns to hell.

7 How excellent his love,
Whence all our safety springs!

O never let my soul remove
From underneath his wings.

Psalm 37:1. 1-15. First Part. The cure of envy,
fretfulness, and unbelief; or, The rewards of the
righteous, and the wicked; or, The world's
hatred, and the saint's patience.

1 Why should I vex my soul and fret
To see the wicked rise?
Or envy sinners waxing great,
By violence and lies.

2 As flowery grass cut down at noon,
Before the evening fades
So shall their glories vanish soon
In everlasting shades.

3 Then let me make the Lord my trust,
And practise all that's good;
So shall I dwell among the just,
And he'll provide me food.

4 I to my God my ways commit,
And cheerful wait his will;
Thy hand, which guides my doubtful feet,
Shall my desires fulfil.

3 Mine innocence shalt thou display,
And make thy judgments known,
Fair as the light of dawning day,
And glorious as the noon.

6 The meek at last the earth possess,
And are the heirs of heav'n;
True riches with abundant peace,
To humble souls are given.

PAUSE.

7 Rest in the Lord and keep his way,
Nor let your anger rise,
Tho' providence should long delay
To punish haughty vice.

8 Let sinners join to break your peace,
And plot, and rage, and foam;
The Lord derides them, for he sees
Their day of vengeance come.

9 They have drawn out the threatening sword,
Have bent the murderous bow,
To slay the men that fear the Lord,
And bring the righteous low.

10 My God shall break their bows, and burn
Their persecuting darts,
Shall their own swords against them turn,
And pain surprise their hearts.

Psalm 37:2. 16 21 26-31. Second Part.
Charity to the poor; or, Religion in words and
deeds.

1 Why do the wealthy wicked boast,
And grow profanely bold?
The meanest portion of the just
Excels the sinner's gold.

2 The wicked borrows of his friends,
But ne'er designs to pay;
The saint is merciful and lends,
Nor turns the poor away.

3 His alms with liberal heart he gives
Amongst the sons of need;
His memory to long ages lives,
And blessed is his seed.

4 His lips abhor to talk profane,
To slander or defraud;
His ready tongue declares to men
What he has learn'd of God.

5 The law and gospel of the Lord
Deep in his heart abide;
Led by the Spirit and the word,
His feet shall never slide.

6 When sinners fall, the righteous stand,
Preserv'd from every snare;
They shall possess the promis'd land,
And dwell for ever there.

Psalm 37:3. 23-27. Third Part.
The way and end of the righteous and the
wicked.

1 My God, the steps of pious men
Are order'd by thy will;
Tho' they should fall, they rise again,
Thy hand supports them still.

2 The Lord delights to see their ways,
Their virtue he approves;
He'll ne'er deprive them of his grace,
Nor leave the men he loves.

3 The heavenly heritage is theirs,
Their portion and their home;
He feeds them now, and makes them heirs
Of blessings long to come.

4 Wait on the Lord, ye sons of men,
Nor fear when tyrants frown;
Ye shall confess their pride was vain,
When justice casts them down.

PAUSE.

5 The haughty sinner have I seen,
Nor fearing man nor God,
Like a tall bay-tree fair and green,
Spreading his arms abroad.

6 And lo! he vanish'd from the ground,
Destroy'd by hands unseen:
Nor root, nor branch, nor leaf was found
Where all that pride had been.

7 But mark the man of righteousness,
His several steps attend;
True pleasure runs thro' all his ways,
And peaceful is his end.

Psalm 38. Guilt of conscience and relief; or,
Repentance, and prayer for pardon and health.

1 Amidst thy wrath remember love,
Restore thy servant, Lord;
Nor let a father's chastening prove
Like an avenger's sword.

2 Thine arrows stick within my heart,
My flesh is sorely prest;
Between the sorrow and the smart
My spirit finds no rest.

3 My sins a heavy load appear,
And o'er my head are gone;
Too heavy they for me to bear,
Too hard for me t' atone.

4 My thoughts are like a troubled sea,
My head still bending down;
And I go mourning all the day
Beneath my Father's frown.

5 Lord, I am weak, and broken sore,
None of my powers are whole;
The inward anguish makes me roar,
The anguish of my soul.

6 All my desire to thee is known,
Thine eye counts every tear,
And every sigh, and every groan
Is notic'd by thine ear.

7 Thou art my God, my only hope;
My God will hear my cry;
My God will bear my spirit up
When Satan bids me die.

8 [My foot is ever apt to slide,
My foes rejoice to see't;
They raise their pleasure and their pride
When they supplant my feet.

9 But I'll confess my guilt to thee,
And grieve for all my sin,
I'll mourn how weak my graces be,
And beg support divine.

10 My God, forgive my follies past,
And be for ever nigh;
O Lord of my salvation, haste,
Before thy servant die.]

Psalm 39:1. 1 2 3. First Part. Watchfulness over
the tongue; or, Prudence and zeal.

1 Thus I resolv'd before the Lord,
"Now will I watch my tongue,
"Lest I let slip one sinful word,
"Or do my neighbour wrong."

2 And if I'm e'er constrain'd to stay
With men of lives profane

I'll set a double guard that day,
Nor let my talk be vain.

3 I'll scarce allow my lips to speak
The pious thoughts I feel,
Lest scoffers should th' occasion take
To mock my holy zeal.

4 Yet if some proper hour appear,
I'll not be overaw'd,
But let the scoffing sinners hear
That I can speak for God.

Psalm 39:2. 4-7. Second Part.
The vanity of man as mortal.

1 Teach me the measure of my days,
Thou maker of my frame;
I would survey life's narrow space,
And learn' how frail I am.

2 A span is all that we can boast,
An inch or two of time;
Man is but vanity and dust
In all his flower and prime.

3 See the vain race of mortals move
Like shadows o'er the plain;
They rage and strive, desire and love,
But all the noise is vain.

4 Some walk in honour's gaudy show,
Some dig for golden ore,
They toil for heirs, they know not who,
And straight are seen no more.

5 What should I wish or wait for then
From creatures, earth and dust?
They make our expectations vain,
And disappoint our trust.

6 Now I forbid my carnal hope,
My fond desires recall;
I give my mortal interest up,
And make my God my all.

Psalm 39:3. 9-13. Third Part.
Sick-bed devotion; or, Pleading without
repining.

1 God of my life, look gently down,
Behold the pains I feel;
But I am dumb before thy throne,
Nor dare dispute thy will.

2 Diseases are thy servants, Lord,
They come at thy command;
I'll not attempt a murmuring word
Against thy chastening hand.

3 Yet I may plead with humble cries,
Remove thy sharp rebukes;
My strength consumes, my spirit dies
Thro' thy repeated strokes.

4 Crush'd as a moth beneath thy hand,
We moulder to the dust;
Our feeble powers can ne'er withstand,
And all our beauty's lost.

5 [This mortal life decays apace,
How soon the bubble's broke!
Adam and all his numerous race
Are vanity and smoke.]

6 I'm but a sojourner below,
As all my fathers were,
May I be well prepar'd to go
When I the summons hear.

7 But if my life be spar'd awhile,
Before my last remove,
Thy praise shall be my business still,
And I'll declare thy love.

Psalm 40:1. 1 3 5 17. First Part. C. M.
A song of deliverance from great distress.

1 I waited patient for the Lord,
He bow'd to hear my cry;
He saw me resting on his word,
And brought salvation nigh.

2 He rais'd me from a horrid pit
Where mourning long I lay,
And from my bonds releas'd my feet,
Deep bonds of miry clay.

3 Firm on a rock he made me stand,
And taught my cheerful tongue

To praise the wonders of his hand,
In a new thankful song.

4 I'll spread his works of grace abroad;
The saints with joy shall hear,
And sinners learn to make my God
Their only hope and fear.

5 How many are thy thoughts of love!
Thy mercies, Lord, how great!
We have not words nor hours enough
Their numbers to repeat.

6 When I'm afflicted, poor and low,
And light and peace depart,
My God beholds my heavy woe,
And bears me on his heart.

Psalm 40:2. 6-9. Second Part. C. M.
The incarnation and sacrifice of Christ.

1 Thus saith the Lord,
"Your work is vain,
"Give your burnt offerings o'er,
"In dying goats and bullocks slain
"My soul delights no more."

2 Then spake the Saviour, "Lo, I'm here,
"My God, to do thy will;
"'Whate'er thy sacred books declare,
"Thy servant shall fulfil.

3 "Thy law is ever in my sight,
"I keep it near my heart;
"Mine ears are open'd with delight
"To what thy lips impart."

4 And see the bless'd Redeemer comes,
Th' eternal Son appears,
And at th' appointed time assumes
The body God prepares.

5 Much he reveal'd his Father's grace,
And much his truth he shew'd,
And preach'd the way of righteousness,
Where great assemblies stood.

6 His Father's honour touch'd his heart,
He pity'd sinners' cries,

And, to fulfil a Saviour's part,
Was made a sacrifice,

PAUSE.

7 No blood of beasts on altars shed
Could wash the conscience clean,
But the rich sacrifice he paid
Atones for all our sin.

8 Then was the great salvation spread,
And Satan's kingdom shook;
Thus by the woman's promis'd seed
The serpent's head was broke.

Psalm 40:3. 5-10. L. M.
Christ our sacrifice.

1 The wonders, Lord, thy love has wrought,
Exceed our praise, surmount our thought;
Should I attempt the long detail,
My speech would faint, my numbers fail.

2 No blood of beasts on altars spilt,
Can cleanse the souls of men from guilt,
But thou hast set before our eyes
An all-sufficient sacrifice.

3 Lo! thine eternal Son appears,
To thy designs he bows his ears,
Assumes a body, well prepar'd,
And well performs a work so hard.

4 "Behold, I come," (the Saviour cries,
With love and duty in his eyes)
"I come to bear the heavy load
"Of sins, and do thy will, my God.

5 "'Tis written in thy great decree,
"'Tis in thy book foretold of me,
"I must fulfil the Saviour's part,
"And, lo! thy law is in my heart!

6 "I'll magnify thy holy law,
"And rebels to obedience draw,
"'When on my cross I'm lifted high,
"Or to my crown above the sky.

7 "The Spirit shall descend, and show
"What thou hast done, and what I do;

"The wond'ring world shall learn thy grace,
"Thy wisdom and thy righteousness."

Psalm 41. 1 2 3.
Charity to the poor; or, Pity to the afflicted.

1 Blest is the man whose bowels move,
And melt with pity to the poor,
Whose soul, by sympathising love,
Feels what his fellow-saints endure.

2 His heart contrives for their relief
More good than his own hands can do;
He, in the time of general grief,
Shall find the Lord has bowels too.

3 His soul shall live secure on earth,
With secret blessings on his head,
When drought, and pestilence, and dearth
Around him multiply their dead.

4 Or if he languish on his couch,
God will pronounce his sins forgiv'n,
Will save him with a healing touch,
Or take his willing soul to heaven.

Psalm 42:1. 1-5. First Part. Desertion and hope;
or, Complaint of absence from public worship.

1 With earnest longings of the mind,
My God, to thee I look;
So pants the hunted hart to find
And taste the cooling brook.

2 When shall I see thy courts of grace,
And meet my God again?
So long an absence from thy face
My heart endures with pain.

3 Temptations vex my weary soul,
And tears are my repast;
The foe insults without control,
"And where's your God at last?"

4 'Tis with a mournful pleasure now
I think on ancient days;
Then to thy house did numbers go,
And all our work was praise.

5 But why, my soul, sunk down so far
Beneath this heavy load?
Why do my thoughts indulge despair,
And sin against my God?

6 Hope in the Lord, whose mighty hand
Can all thy woes remove;
For I shall yet before him stand,
And sing restoring love.

Psalm 42:2. 6-11. Second Part. Melancholy
thoughts reproved; or, Hope in afflictions.

1 My spirit sinks within me, Lord,
But I will call thy name to mind,
And times of past distress record,
When I have found my God was kind.

2 Huge troubles, with tumultuous noise,
Swell like a sea, and round me spread;
Thy water-spouts drown all my joys,
And rising waves roll o'er my head.

3 Yet will the Lord command his love,
When I address his throne by day,
Nor in the night his grace remove;
The night shall hear me sing and pray.

4 I'll cast myself before his feet,
And say "My God, my heavenly Rock,
"Why doth thy love so long forget
"The soul that groans beneath thy stroke?"

5 I'll chide my heart that sinks so low,
Why should my soul indulge her grief?
Hope in the Lord, and praise him too,
He is my rest, my sure relief.

6 Thy light and truth shall guide me still,
Thy word shall my best thoughts employ,
And lead me to thine heavenly hill,
My God, my most exceeding Joy.

Psalm 44. 1 2 3 8 15-26.
The church's complaint in persecution.

1 Lord, we have heard thy works of old,
Thy works of power and grace,

When to our ears our fathers told
The wonders of their days:

2 How thou didst build thy churches here,
And make thy gospel known;
Amongst them did thine arm appear,
Thy light and glory shone.

3 In God they boasted all the day,
And in a cheerful throng
Did thousands meet to praise and pray,
And grace was all their song.

4 But now our souls are seiz'd with shame,
Confusion fills our face,
To hear the enemy blaspheme,
And fools reproach thy grace.

5 Yet have we not forgot our God,
Nor falsely dealt with heaven,
Nor have our steps declin'd the road
Of duty thou hast given.

6 Tho' dragons all around us roar
With their destructive breath,
And thine own hand has bruis'd us sore
Hard by the gates of death.

PAUSE.

7 We are expos'd all day to die
As martyrs for thy cause,
As sheep for slaughter bound we lie
By sharp and bloody laws.

8 Awake, arise, almighty Lord,
Why sleeps thy wonted grace?
Why should we look like men abhorr'd,
Or banish'd from thy face?

9 Wilt thou for ever cast us off
And still neglect our cries?
For ever hide thine heavenly love
From our afflicted eyes?

10 Down to the dust our soul is bow'd,
And dies upon the ground;
Rise for our help, rebuke the proud,
And all their powers confound.

11 Redeem us from perpetual shame,
Our Saviour and our God;
We plead the honours of thy Name,
The merits of thy blood.

Psalm 45:1. S. M. The glory of Christ; the
success of the gospel; and the Gentile church.

1 My Saviour and my King,
Thy beauties are divine;
Thy lips with blessings overflow,
And every grace is thine.

2 Now make thy glory known,
Gird on thy dreadful sword,
And ride in majesty to spread
The conquests of thy word.

Strike thro' thy stubborn foes,
Or melt their hearts t'obey,
While justice, meekness, grace, and truth,
Attend thy glorious way.

4 Thy laws, O God, are right;
Thy throne shall ever end;
And thy victorious gospel proves
A sceptre in thy hand.

5 [Thy Father and thy God
Hath without measure shed
His Spirit, like a joyful oil,
T'anoint thy sacred head.]

6 [Behold, at thy right hand
The Gentile church is seen,
Like a fair bride in rich attire,
And princes guard the queen.]

7 Fair bride, receive his love,
Forget thy father's house;
Forsake thy gods, thy idol gods,
And pay thy Lord thy vows.

8 O let thy God and King
Thy sweetest thoughts employ;
Thy children shall his honours sing
In palaces of joy.

Psalm 45:2. C. M.
The personal glories and government of Christ.

1 I'll speak the honours of my King,
His form divinely fair;
None of the sons of mortal race
May with the Lord compare.

2 Sweet is thy speech and heavenly grace
Upon thy lips is shed;
Thy God, with blessings infinite,
Hath crown'd thy sacred head.

3 Gird on thy sword, victorious Prince,
Ride with majestic sway;
Thy terrors shall strike thro' thy foes,
And make the world obey.

4 Thy throne, O God, for ever stands;
Thy word of grace shall prove
A peaceful sceptre in thy hands,
To rule the saints by love.

5 Justice and truth attend thee still
But mercy is thy choice;
And God, thy God, thy soul shall fill
With most peculiar joys.

Psalm 45:3. First Part. L. M.
The glory of Christ, and power of his gospel.

1 Now be my heart inspir'd to sing
The glories of my Saviour-king,
Jesus the Lord; how heavenly fair
His form! how 'bright his beauties are!

2 O'er all the sons of human race
He shines with a superior grace,
Love from his lips divinely flows,
And blessings all his state compose.

3 Dress thee in arms, most mighty Lord,
Gird on the terror of thy sword,
In majesty and glory ride
With truth and meekness at thy side.

4 Thine anger, like a pointed dart,
Shall pierce the foes of stubborn heart;
Or words of mercy kind and sweet
Shall melt the rebels at thy feet.

5 Thy throne, O God, for ever stands,
Grace is the sceptre in thy hands;
Thy laws and works are just and right,
Justice and grace are thy delight.

6 God, thine own God, has richly shed
His oil of gladness on thy head,
And with his sacred Spirit blest
His first-born Son above the rest.

Psalm 45:4. Second Part. L. M.
Christ and his church; or, The mystical
marriage.

1 The king of saints, how fair his face,
Adorn'd with majesty and grace!
He comes with blessings from above,
And wins the nations to his love.

2 At his right hand our eyes behold
The queen array'd in purest gold;
The world admires her heavenly dress,
Her robe of joy and righteousness.

3 He forms her beauties like his own;
He calls and seats her near his throne:
Fair stranger, let thine heart forget
The idols of thy native state.

4 So shall the King the more rejoice
In thee, the favourite of his choice;
Let him be lov'd and yet ador'd,
For he's thy Maker and thy Lord.

5 O happy hour, when thou shalt rise
To his fair palace in the skies,
And all thy Sons (a numerous train)
Each like a prince in glory reign!

6 Let endless honours crown his head;
Let every age his praises spread;
While we with cheerful songs approve
The condescensions of his love.

Psalm 46:1. First Part. The church's safety and
triumph among national desolations.

1 God is the refuge of his saints,
When storms of sharp distress invade;

Ere we can offer our complaints
Behold him present with his aid.

2 Let mountains from their seats be hurl'd
Down to the deep, and buried there;
Convulsions shake the solid world,
Our faith shall never yield to fear.

3 Loud may the troubled ocean roar,
In sacred peace our souls abide,
While every nation, every shore,
Trembles, and dreads the swelling tide.

4 There is a stream whose gentle flow
Supplies the city of our God;
Life, love, and joy still gliding thro',
And watering our divine abode.

5 That sacred stream, thine holy word,
That all our raging fear controls:
Sweet peace thy promises afford,
And give new strength to fainting souls.

6 Sion enjoys her monarch's love,
Secure against a threatening hour;
Nor can her firm foundations move,
Built on his truth, and arm'd with pow'r.

Psalm 46:2. Second Part.
God fights for his church.

1 Let Sion in her King rejoice,
Tho' tyrants rage and kingdoms rise;
He utters his almighty voice,
The nations melt, the tumult dies.

2 The Lord of old for Jacob fought,
And Jacob's God is still our aid;
Behold the works his hand has wrought,
What desolations he has made!

3 From sea to sea, thro' all the shores,
He makes the noise of battle cease;
When from on high his thunder roars,
He awes the trembling world to peace.

4 He breaks the bow, he cuts the spear,
Chariots he burns with heavenly flame;
Keep silence all the earth, and hear
The sound and glory of his Name.

5 "Be still, and learn that I am God,
"I'll be exalted o'er the lands,
"I will be known and fear'd abroad,
"But still my throne in Sion stands."

6 O Lord of hosts, almighty King,
While we so near thy presence dwell,
Our faith shall sit secure, and sing
Defiance to the gates of hell.

Psalm 47.
Christ ascending and reigning.

1 O for a shout of sacred joy
To God the sovereign King!
Let every land their tongues employ,
And hymns of triumph sing.

2 Jesus our God ascends on high,
His heavenly guards around
Attend him rising thro' the sky,
With trumpet's joyful sound.

3 While angels shout and praise their King,
Let mortals learn their strains;
Let all the earth his honour sing;
O'er all the earth he reigns.

4 Rehearse his praise with awe profound,
Let knowledge lead the song,
Nor mock him with a solemn sound
Upon a thoughtless tongue.

5 In Israel stood his ancient throne,
He lov'd that chosen race;
But now he calls the world his own,
And heathens taste his grace.

6 The British islands are the Lord's,
There Abraham's God is known,
While powers and princes, shields and swords,
Submit before his throne.

Psalm 48:1. 1-8. First Part.
The church is the honour and safety of a nation.

1 [Great is the Lord our God,
And let his praise be great;

He makes his churches his abode,
His most delightful seat.

2 These temples of his grace,
How beautiful they stand!
The honours of our native place,
And bulwarks of our land.]

3 In Sion God is known
A refuge in distress;
How bright has his salvation shone
Thro' all her palaces!

4 When kings against her join'd,
And saw the Lord was there,
In wild confusion of the mind
They fled with hasty tear.

5 When navies tall and proud
Attempt to spoil our peace,
He sends his tempests roaring loud,
And sinks them in the seas.

6 Oft have our fathers told,
Our eyes have often seen,
How well our God secures the fold
Where his own sheep have been.

7 In every new distress
We'll to his house repair.
We'll think upon his wondrous grace,
And seek deliverance there.

Psalm 48:2. 10-14. Second Part.
The beauty of the church; or,
Gospel worship and order.

1 Far as thy name is known
The world declares thy praise;
Thy saints, O Lord, before thy throne
Their songs of honour raise.

2 With joy let Judah stand
On Sion's chosen hill,
Proclaim the wonders of thy hand,
And counsels of thy will.

3 Let strangers walk around
The city where we dwell,

Compass and view thine holy ground,
And mark the building well.

4 The orders of thy house,
The worship of thy court,
The cheerful songs, the solemn vows;
And make a fair report.

5 How decent and how wise!
How glorious to behold!
Beyond the pomp that charms the eyes,
And rites adorn'd with gold.

6 The God we worship now
Will guide us till we die,
Will be our God while here below,
And ours above the sky.

Psalm 49:1. 8-14. First Part. C. M.
Pride and death; or, The vanity of life and
riches.

1 Why doth the man of riches grow
To insolence and pride,
To see his wealth and honours flow
With every rising tide?

2 [Why doth he treat the poor with scorn,
Made of the self-same clay,
And boast as tho' his flesh was born
Of better dust than they?]

3 Not all his treasures can procure
His soul a short reprieve,
Redeem from death one guilty hour,
Or make his brother live.

4 [Life is a blessing can't be sold,
The ransom is too high;
Justice will ne'er be brib'd with gold
That man may never die.]

5 He sees the brutish and the wise,
The timorous and the brave,
Quit their possessions, close their eyes,
And hasten to the grave.

6 Yet 'tis his inward thought and pride,—
"My house shall ever stand;

"And that my name may long abide,
"I'll give it to my land."

7 Vain are his thoughts, his hopes are lost,
How soon his memory dies!
His name is written in the dust
Where his own carcase lies.

PAUSE.

8 This is the folly of their way;
And yet their sons, as vain,
Approve the words their fathers say,
And act their works again.

9 Men void of wisdom and of grace,
If honour raise them high.
Live like the beast, a thoughtless race,
And like the beast they die.

10 Laid in the grave like silly sheep,
Death feeds upon them there,
Till the last trumpet break their sleep
In terror and despair.

Psalm 49:2. 14 15. Second Part. C. M.
Death and the resurrection.

1 Ye sons of pride, that hate the just,
And trample on the poor,
When death has brought you down to dust,
Your pomp shall rise no more,

2 The last great day shall change the scene;
When will that hour appear?
When shall the just revive, and reign
O'er all that scorn'd them here?

3 God will my naked soul receive,
When sep'rate from the flesh;
And break the prison of the grave
To raise my bones afresh.

4 Heaven is my everlasting home,
Th' inheritance is sure;
Let men of pride their rage resume,
But I'll repine no more.

Psalm 49:3. L. M.
The rich sinner's death, and the saint's resurrection.

1 Why do the proud insult the poor,
And boast the large estates they have?
How vain are riches to secure
Their haughty owners from the grave!

2 They can't redeem one hour from death,
With all the wealth in which they trust;
Nor give a dying brother breath,
When God commands him down to dust.

3 There the dark earth and dismal shade
Shall clasp their naked bodies round;
That flesh, so delicately fed,
Lies cold, and moulders in the ground.

4 Like thoughtless sheep the sinner dies,
Laid in the grave for worms to eat;
The saints shall in the morning rise,
And find th' oppressor at their feet.

5 His honours perish in the dust,
And pomp and beauty, birth and blood:
That glorious day exalts the just
To full dominion o'er the proud.

6 My Saviour shall my life restore,
And raise me from my dark abode;
My flesh and soul shall part no more,
But dwell for ever near my God.

Psalm 50:1. 1-6. First Part. C. M.
The last judgment; or, The saints rewarded.

1 The Lord, the Judge, before his throne,
Bids the whole earth draw nigh,
The nations near the rising sun,
And near the western sky.

2 No more shall bold blasphemers say,
"Judgment will ne'er begin,"
No more abuse his long delay
To impudence and sin.

3 Thron'd on a cloud our God shall come,
Bright flames prepare his way,

Thunder and darkness, fire and storm,
Lead on the dreadful day.

4 Heaven from above his call shall hear,
Attending angels come,
And earth and hell shall know and fear
His justice and their doom.

5 "But gather all my saints," he cries,
"That made their peace with God,
"By the Redeemer's sacrifice,
"And seal'd it with his blood.

6 "Their faith and works brought forth to light
"Shall make the world confess
"My sentence of reward is right,
"And heaven adore my grace."

Psalm 50:2. 8 10 11 14 15 23.
Second Part. C. M.
Obedience is better than sacrifice.

1 Thus saith the Lord, "the spacious fields
"And flocks and herds are mine
"O'er all the cattle of the hills
"I claim a right divine.

2 "I ask no sheep for sacrifice,
"Nor bullocks burnt with fire;
"To hope and love, to pray and praise,
"Is all that I require.

3 "Call upon me when trouble's near,
"My hand shall set thee free;
"Then shall thy thankful lips declare
"The honour due to me.

4 "The man that offers humble praise,
"He glorifies me best;
"And those that tread my holy ways
"Shall my salvation taste."

Psalm 50:3. 1 5 8 16 21 22. 3d Part. C. M.
The judgement of hypocrites.

1 When Christ to judgment shall descend
And saints surround their Lord,
He calls the nations to attend,
And hear his awful word.

2 "Not for the want of bullocks slain
"Will I the world reprove;
"Altars and rites and forms are vain,
"Without the fire of love.

3 "And what have hypocrites to do
"To bring their sacrifice?
"They call my statutes just and true,
"But deal in theft and lies.

4 "Could you expect to 'scape my sight,
"And sin without control?
"But I shall bring your crimes to light,
"With anguish in your soul."

5 Consider, ye that slight the Lord,
Before his wrath appear;
If once you fall beneath his sword,
There's no deliverer there.

Psalm 50:4. L. M.
Hypocrisy exposed.

1 The Lord, the Judge, his churches warns,
Let hypocrites attend and fear,
Who place their hope in rites and forms,
But make not faith nor love their care.

2 Vile wretches dare rehearse his name
With lips of falsehood and deceit;
A friend or brother they defame,
And soothe and flatter those they hate.

3 They watch to do their neighbours wrong;
Yet dare to seek their Maker's face;
They take his covenant on their tongue,
But break his laws, abuse his grace.

4 To heaven they lift their hands unclean,
Defil'd with lust, defil'd with blood;
By night they practise every sin,
By day their mouths draw near to God.

5 And while his judgments long delay,
They grow secure and sin the more;
They think he sleeps as well as they,
And put far off the dreadful hour.

6 O dreadful hour! when God draws near,
And sets their crimes before their eyes!

His wrath their guilty souls shall tear,
And no deliverer dare to rise.

Psalm 50:5. To a new Tune.
The last judgment.

1 The Lord the Sovereign sends his summons
forth,
Calls the south nations, and awakes the north;
From east to west the sounding orders spread
Thro' distant worlds and regions of the dead:
No more shall atheists mock his long delay;
His vengeance sleeps no more: behold the day!

2 Behold the Judge descends; his guards are
nigh;
Tempest and fire attend him down the sky:
Heaven, earth and hell draw near; let all things
come
To hear his justice and the sinners doom:
But gather first my saints (the Judge commands)
Bring them, ye angels, from their distant lands.

3 Behold! my covenant stands for ever good,
Seal'd by the eternal sacrifice in blood,
And sign'd with all their names; the Greek, the
Jew,
That paid the ancient worship or the new.
There's no distinction here: come spread their
thrones,
And near me seat my favorites and my sons.

4 I their almighty Saviour and their God,
I am their Judge: ye heavens, proclaim abroad
My just eternal sentence, and declare
Those awful truths that sinners dread to hear:
Sinners in Zion, tremble and retire;
I doom the painted hypocrite to fire.

5 Not for the want of goats or bullocks slain
Do I condemn thee; bulls and goats are vain
Without the flames of love: in vain the store
Of brutal offerings that were mine before;
Mine are the tamer beasts and savage breed,
Flocks, herds, and fields, and forests where they
feed.

6 If I were hungry would I ask thee food?
When did I thirst, or drink thy bullocks blood?
Can I be flatter'd with thy cringing bows,

Thy solemn chatterings and fantastic vows?
Are my eyes charm'd thy vestments to behold,
Glaring in gems, and gay in woven gold?

7 Unthinking wretch! how couldst thou hope to please
A God, a spirit, with such toys as these?
While with my grace and statutes on thy tongue,
Thou lov'st deceit, and dost thy brother wrong;
In vain to pious forms thy zeal pretends,
Thieves and adulterers are thy chosen friends.

8 Silent I waited with lone-suffering love,
But didst thou hope that I should ne'er reprove?
And cherish such an impious thought within,
That God the righteous would indulge thy sin?
Behold my terrors now: my thunders roll,
And thy own crimes affright thy guilty soul.

9 Sinners, awake betimes; ye fools, be wise;
Awake, before this dreadful morning rise;
Change your vain thoughts, your crooked works amend,
Fly to the Saviour, make the Judge your friend;
Lest like a lion his last vengeance tear
Your trembling souls, and no deliverer near.

Psalm 50:6. To the old proper Tune.
The last judgment.

1 The God of glory sends his summons forth,
Calls the south nations, and awakes the north;
From east to west the sov'reign orders spread,
Thro' distant worlds, and regions of the dead:
The trumpet sounds; hell trembles; heaven rejoices;
Lift up your heads, ye saints, with cheerful voices.

2 No more shall atheists mock his long delay;
His vengeance sleeps no more; behold the day;
Behold the Judge descends; his guards are nigh;
Tempests and fire attend him down the sky.
When God appears, all nature shall adore him;
While sinners tremble, saints rejoice before him,

3 "Heaven, earth, and hell, draw near; let all things come
"To hear my justice and the sinner's doom;
"But gather first my saints," the Judge

commands,
"Bring them, ye angels from their distant lands:"
When Christ returns, wake every cheerful passion,
And shout, ye saints; he comes for your salvation.

4 "Behold my covenant stands for ever good,
"Seal'd by th' eternal sacrifice in blood,
"And sign'd with all their names, the Greek, the Jew,
"That paid the ancient worship or the new."
There's no distinction here: join all your voices,
And raise your heads, ye saints, for heaven rejoices.

5 "Here (saith the Lord) ye angels, spread their thrones:
"And near me seat my favorites and my sons:
"Come, my redeem'd, possess the joys prepar'd
"Ere time began! 'tis your divine reward:"
When Christ returns, wake every cheerful passion,
And shout, ye saints; he comes for your salvation.

PAUSE THE FIRST.

6 "I am the Saviour, I th' almighty God,
"I am the Judge: ye heavens, proclaim abroad
"My just eternal sentence, and declare
"Those awful truths that sinners dread to hear,"
When God appears all nature shall adore him;
While sinners tremble, saints rejoice before him.

7 "Stand forth, thou bold blasphemer and profane,
"Now feel my wrath, nor call my threatenings vain,
"Thou hypocrite, once drest in saint's attire,
"I doom the painted hypocrite to fire."
Judgment proceeds; hell trembles; heaven rejoices;
Lift up your heads, ye saints, with cheerful voices.

8 "Not for the want of goats or bullocks slain
"Do I condemn thee; bulls and goats are vain
"Without the flames of love; in vain the store
"Of brutal offerings that were mine before:"
Earth is the Lord's; all nature shall adore him;
While sinners tremble, saints rejoice before him.

9 "If I were hungry, would I ask thee food?
"When did I thirst, or drink thy bullocks blood?
"Mine are the tamer beasts and savage breed,
"Flocks, herds, and fields, and forests where
they feed:"
All is the Lord's; he rules the wide creation:
Gives sinners vengeance, and the saints
salvation.

10 "Can I be flatter'd with thy cringing bows,
"Thy solemn chatterings and fantastic vows?
"Are my eyes charm'd thy vestments to behold,
"Glaring in gems, and gay in woven gold?"
God is the judge of hearts; no fair disguises
Can screen the guilty when his vengeance rises.

PAUSE THE SECOND.

11 "Unthinking wretch! how couldst thou hope
to please
"A God, a spirit with such toys as these!
"While with my grace and statutes on thy
tongue,
"Thou lov'st deceit, and dost thy brother
wrong!"
Judgment proceeds; hell trembles; heaven
rejoices:
Lift up your heads, ye saints, with cheerful
voices.

12 "In vain to pious forms thy zeal pretends,
"Thieves and adulterers are thy chosen friends;
"While the false flatterer at my altar waits,
"His harden'd soul divine instruction hates."
God is the judge of hearts; no fair disguises
Can screen the guilty when his vengeance rises.

13 "Silent I waited with long suffering love;
"But didst thou hope that I should ne'er reprove?
"And cherish such an impious thought within,
"That the All-Holy would indulge thy sin?"
See, God appears; all nature joins t' adore him;
Judgment proceeds, and sinners fall before him.

14 "Behold my terrors now; my thunders roll,
"And thy own crimes affright thy guilty soul;
"Now like a lion shall my vengeance tear
"Thy bleeding heart, and no deliverer near:"
Judgment concludes; hell trembles; heaven
rejoices;
Lift up your heads, ye saints, with cheerful
voices..

EPIPHONEMA.

15 Sinners, awake betimes; ye fools, be wise;
Awake before this dreadful morning rise:
Change your vain thoughts, your crooked works
amend,
Fly to the Saviour, make the Judge your friend:
Then join the saints: wake every cheerful
passion;
When Christ returns, he comes for your
salvation.

Psalm 51:1. First Part. L. M.
A penitent pleading for pardon.

1 Shew pity, Lord, O Lord, forgive,
Let a repenting rebel live:
Are not thy mercies large and free?
May not a sinner trust in thee?

2 My crimes are great, but not surpass
The power and glory of thy grace;
Great God, thy nature hath no bound,
So let thy pardoning love be found.

3 O wash my Soul from every sin,
And make my guilty conscience clean;
Here on my heart the burden lies,
And past offences pain my eyes.

4 My lips with shame my sins confess
Against thy law, against thy grace:
Lord, should thy judgment grow severe,
I am condemn'd, but thou art clear.

5 Should sudden vengeance seize my breath,
I must pronounce thee just in death;
And if my soul were sent to hell,
Thy righteous law approves it well.

6 Yet save a trembling sinner, Lord,
Whose hope, still hovering round thy word,
Would light on some sweet promise there,
Some sure support against despair.

Psalms 51:2. Second Part. L. M.
Original and actual sin confessed.

1 Lord, I am vile, conceiv'd in sin;
And born unholy and unclean;
Sprung from the man whose guilty fall
Corrupts the race, and taints us all.

2 Soon as we draw our infant-breath,
The seeds of sin grow up for death;
Thy law demands a perfect heart,
But we're defil'd in every part.

3 [Great God, create my heart anew,
And form my spirit pure and true:
O make me wise betimes to spy
My danger, and my remedy.]

4 Behold I fall before thy face;
My only refuge is thy grace:
No outward forms can make me clean;
The leprosy lies deep within.

5 No bleeding bird, nor bleeding beast,
Nor hyssop branch, nor sprinkling priest,
Nor running brook, nor flood, nor sea,
Can wash the dismal stain away.

6 Jesus, my God, thy blood alone
Hath power sufficient to atone;
Thy blood can make me white as snow;
No Jewish types could cleanse me so.

7 While guilt disturbs and breaks my peace,
Nor flesh, nor soul hath rest or ease;
Lord, let me hear thy pardoning voice,
And make my broken bones rejoice.

Psalm 51:3. Third Part. L. M. The backslider
restored; or, Repentance and faith in the blood
of Christ.

1 O thou that hear'st when sinners cry,
Tho' all my crimes before thee lie,
Behold them not with angry look,
But blot their memory from thy book.

2 Create my nature pure within,
And form my soul averse to sin;
Let thy good Spirit ne'er depart,
Nor hide thy presence from my heart.

3 I cannot live without thy light,
Cast out and banish'd from thy sight:
Thine holy joys, my God, restore,
And guard me that I fall no more.

4 Tho' I have griev'd thy Spirit, Lord,
His help and comfort still afford:
And let a wretch come near thy throne
To plead the merits of thy Son.

5 A broken heart, my God, my King,
Is all the sacrifice I bring;
The God of grace will ne'er despise
A broken heart for sacrifice.

6 My soul lies humbled in the dust,
And owns thy dreadful sentence just;
Look down, O Lord, with pitying eye,
And save the soul condemn'd to die.

7 Then will I teach the world thy ways;
Sinners shall learn thy sovereign grace;
I'll lead them to my Saviour's blood,
And they shall praise a pardoning God.

8 O may thy love inspire my tongue!
Salvation shall be all my song;
And all my powers shall join to bless
The Lord, my strength and righteousness.

Psalm 51:4. 3-13. First Part. C. M.
Original and actual sin confessed and pardoned.

1 Lord, I would spread my sore distress
And guilt before thine eyes;
Against thy laws, against thy grace,
How high my crimes arise.

2 Shouldst thou condemn my soul to hell,
And crush my flesh to dust,
Heaven would approve thy vengeance well,
And earth must own it just.

3 I from the stock of Adam came,
Unholy and unclean;
All my original is shame,
And all my nature sin.

4 Born in a world of guilt, I drew
Contagion with my breath;

And, as my days advanc'd, I grew
A juster prey for death.

5 Cleanse me, O Lord, and cheer my soul
With thy forgiving love;
O, make my broken spirit whole,
And bid my pains remove.

6 Let not thy Spirit quite depart,
Nor drive me from thy face;
Create anew my vicious heart,
And fill it with thy grace.

7 Then will I make thy mercy known
Before the sons of men;
Backsliders shall address thy throne,
And turn to God again.

Psalm 51:5. 14-17. Second Part. C. M.
Repentance and faith in the blood of Christ.

1 O God of mercy! hear my call,
My loads of guilt remove;
Break down this separating wall
That bars me from thy love.

2 Give me the presence of thy grace,
Then my rejoicing tongue
Shall speak aloud thy righteousness,
And make thy praise my song.

3 No blood of goats, nor heifers slain,
For sin could e'er atone;
The death of Christ shall still remain
Sufficient and alone.

4 A soul opprest with sin's desert,
My God will ne'er despise;
A humble groan, a broken heart
Is our best sacrifice.

Psalm 53. 4-6.
Victory and deliverance from persecution.

1 Are all the foes of Sion fools,
Who thus devour her saints?
Do they not know her Saviour rules,
And pities her complaints?

2 They shall be seiz'd with sad surprise;
For God's revenging arm
Scatters the bones of them that rise
To do his children harm.

3 In vain the sons of Satan boast
Of armies in array:
When God has first despis'd their host,
They fall an easy prey.

4 O for a word from Sion's King
Her captives to restore!
Jacob with all his tribes shall sing,
And Judah weep no more.

Psalm 55:1. 1-8 16-18 22. C. M.
Support for the afflicted and tempted soul.

1 O God, my refuge, hear my cries,
Behold my flowing tears,
For earth and hell my hurt devise,
And triumph in my fears.

2 Their rage is levell'd at my life,
My soul with guilt they load,
And fill my thoughts with inward strife
To shake my hope in God.

3 With inward pain my heart-strings sound,
I groan with every breath;
Horror and fear beset me round
Amongst the shades of death,

4 O were I like a feather'd dove,
And innocence had wings,
I'd fly, and make a long remove,
From all these restless things.

5 Let me to some wild desert go,
And find a peaceful home,
Where storms of malice never blow,
Temptations never come.

6 Vain hopes, and vain inventions all
To 'scape the rage of hell!
The mighty God on whom I call
Can save me here as well.

PAUSE.

7 By morning light I'll seek his face,
At noon repeat my cry,
The night shall hear me ask his grace,
Nor will he long deny.

8 God shall preserve my soul from fear,
Or shield me when afraid;
Ten thousand angels must appear
If he command their aid.

9 I cast my burdens on the Lord,
The Lord sustains them all;
My courage rests upon his word
That saints shall never fall.

10 My highest hopes shall not be vain,
My lips shall spread his praise;
While cruel and deceitful men
Scarce live out half their days.

Psalm 55:2. 15-17 19 22. S. M.
Dangerous prosperity; or,
Daily devotions encouraged.

1 Let sinners take their course,
And choose the road to death;
But in the worship of my God
I'll spend my daily breath.

2 My thoughts address his throne
When morning brings the light;
I seek his blessing every noon,
And pay my vows at night.

3 Thou wilt regard my cries,
O my eternal God,
While sinners perish in surprise
Beneath thine angry rod.

4 Because they dwell at ease,
And no sad changes feel,
They neither fear nor trust thy Name,
Nor learn to do thy will.

5 But I with all my cares
Will call upon the Lord,
I'll cast my burdens on his arm,
And rest upon his word,

6 His arm shall well sustain
The children of his love;
The ground on which their safety stands
No earthly power can move.

Psalm 56.
Deliverance from oppression and falsehood; or,
God's care of his people, in answer to faith and
prayer.

1 Thou, whose justice reigns on high,
And makes th' oppressor cease,
Behold how envious sinners try
To vex and break my peace!

2 The Sons of violence and lies
Join to devour me, Lord;
But as my hourly dangers rise,
My refuge is thy word.

3 In God most holy, just, and true,
I have repos'd my trust;
Nor will I fear what flesh can do,
The offspring of the dust.

4 They wrest my words to mischief still,
Charge me with unknown faults;
Mischief doth all their councils fill,
And malice all their thoughts.

5 Shall they escape without thy frown?
Must their devices stand?
O cast the haughty sinner down,
And let him know thy hand!

PAUSE.

6 God counts the sorrows of his saints,
Their groans affect his ears;
Thou hast a book for my complaints,
A bottle for my tears.

7 When to thy throne I raise my cry
The wicked fear and flee;
So swift is prayer to reach the sky,
So near is God to me.

8 In thee, most holy, just, and true,
I have repos'd my trust;

Nor will I fear what man can do,
The offspring of the dust.

9 Thy solemn vows are on me, Lord,
Thou shalt receive my praise;
I'll sing, "how faithful is thy word,
"How righteous all thy ways!"

10 Thou hast secur'd my soul from death;
O set thy prisoner free,
That heart and hand, and life and breath
May be employ'd for thee.

Psalm 57.
Praise for protection, grace, and truth.

1 My God, in whom are all the springs
Of boundless love and grace unknown,
Hide me beneath thy spreading wings
Till the dark cloud is overblown.

2 Up to the heavens I send my cry,
The Lord will my desires perform;
He sends his angel from the sky,
And saves me from the threatening storm.

3 Be thou exalted, O my God,
Above the heavens where angels dwell:
Thy power on earth be known abroad,
And land to land thy wonders tell.

4 My heart is fix'd; my song shall raise
Immortal honours to thy Name;
Awake, my tongue, to sound his praise,
My tongue, the glory of my frame.

5 High o'er the earth his mercy reigns,
And reaches to the utmost sky;
His truth to endless years remains,
When lower worlds dissolve and die.

6 Be thou exalted, O my God,
Above the heavens where angels dwell;
Thy power on earth be known abroad,
And land to land thy wonders tell.

Psalm 58. As the 113th Psalm.
Warning to magistrates.

1 Judges, who rule the world by laws,
Will ye despise the righteous cause,
When th' injur'd poor before you stands?
Dare ye condemn the righteous poor,
And let rich sinners 'scape secure,
While gold and greatness bribe your hands?

2 Have ye forgot, or never knew,
That God will judge the judges too?
High in the heavens his justice reigns;
Yet you invade the rights of God,
And send your bold decrees abroad,
To bind the conscience in your chains.

3 A poison'd arrow is your tongue,
The arrow sharp, the poison strong,
And death attends where'er it wounds:
You hear no counsels, cries or tears;
So the deaf adder stops her ears
Against the power of charming sounds.

4 Break out their teeth, eternal God,
Those teeth of lions dy'd in blood;
And crush the serpents in the dust:
As empty chaff when whirlwinds rise,
Before the sweeping tempest flies,
So let their hopes and names be lost.

5 Th' Almighty thunders from the sky,
Their grandeur melts, their titles die,
As hills of snow dissolve and run,
Or snails that perish in their slime,
Or births that come before their time,
Vain births, that never see the sun.

6 Thus shall the vengeance of the Lord
Safety and joy to saints afford;
And all that hear shall join and say,
"Sure there's a God that rules on high,
"A God that hears his children cry,
"And will their sufferings well repay."

Psalm 60. 1-5 10-12.
On a day of humiliation for disappointments in war.

1 Lord, hast thou cast the nation off?
Must we for ever mourn?
Wilt thou indulge immortal wrath?
Shall mercy ne'er return?

2 The terror of one frown of thine
Melts all our strength away;
Like men that totter drunk with wine,
We tremble in dismay.

3 Great Britain shakes beneath thy stroke,
And dreads thy threatening hand;
O heal the island thou hast broke,
Confirm the wavering land.

4 Lift up a banner in the field,
For those that fear thy Name;
Save thy beloved with thy shield,
And put our foes to shame.

5 Go with our armies to the fight,
Like a confederate God;
In vain confederate powers unite
Against thy lifted rod.

6 Our troops shall gain a wide renown
By thine assisting hand;
'Tis God that treads the mighty down,
And makes the feeble stand.

Psalm 61. 1-6.
Safety in God.

1 When overwhelm'd with grief
My heart within me dies,
Helpless and far from all relief
To heaven I lift mine eyes.

2 O lead me to the rock
That's high above my head,
And make the covert of thy wings
My shelter and my shade.

3 Within thy presence, Lord,
For ever I'll abide;
Thou art the tower of my defence,
The refuge where I hide.

4 Thou givest me the lot
Of those that fear thy Name;
If endless life be their reward,
I shall possess the same.

Psalm 62. 5-12.
No trust in the creatures; or,
Faith in divine grace and power.

1 My spirit looks to God alone;
My rock and refuge is his throne;
In all my fears, in all my straits,
My soul on his salvation waits.

2 Trust him, ye saints, in all your ways,
Pour out your hearts before his face:
When helpers fail, and foes invade,
God is our all-sufficient aid.

3 False are the men of high degree,
The baser sort are vanity;
Laid in the balance both appear
Light as a puff of empty air.

4 Make not increasing gold your trust,
Nor set your heart on glittering dust;
Why will you grasp the fleeting smoke;
And not believe what God hath spoke?

5 Once has his awful voice declar'd,
Once and again my ears have heard,
"All power is his eternal due;
"He must be fear'd and trusted too."

6 For sovereign power reigns not alone,
Grace is a partner of the throne:
Thy grace and justice, mighty Lord,
Shall well divide our last reward.

Psalm 63:1. 1 2 5 34. First Part. C. M.
The morning of a Lord's day.

1 Early, my God, without delay
I haste to seek thy face;
My thirsty spirit faints away,
Without thy cheering grace.

2 So pilgrims on the scorching sand,
Beneath a burning sky,
Long for a cooling stream at hand,
And they must drink or die.

3 I've seen thy glory and thy power
Thro' all thy temple shine;

My God, repeat that heavenly hour,
That vision so divine.

4 Not all the blessings of a feast
Can please my soul so well,
As when thy richer grace I taste,
And in thy presence dwell.

5 Not life itself with all her joys,
Can my best passions move,
Or raise so high my cheerful voice
As thy forgiving love.

6 Thus till my last expiring day
I'll bless my God and King;
Thus will I lift my hands to pray,
And tune my lips to sing.

Psalm 63:2. 6-10. Second Part.
Midnight thoughts recollected.

1 'Twas in the watches of the night
I thought upon thy power,
I kept thy lovely face in sight
Amidst the darkest hour.

2 My flesh lay resting on my bed,
My soul arose on high;
"My God, my life, my hope," I said,
"Bring thy salvation nigh."

3 My spirit labours up thine hill,
And climbs the heavenly road;
But thy right hand upholds me still,
While I pursue my God.

4 Thy mercy stretches o'er my head
The shadow of thy wings;
My heart rejoices in thine aid,
My tongue awakes and sings.

5 But the destroyers of my peace
Shall fret and rage in vain;
The tempter shall for ever cease,
And all my sins be slain.

6 Thy sword shall give my foes to death,
And send them down to dwell
In the dark caverns of the earth,
Or to the deeps of hell.

Psalm 63:3. L. M. Longing after God; or, The
love of God better than life.

1 Great God, indulge my humble claim
Thou art my hope, my joy, my rest;
The glories that compose thy Name
Stand all engag'd to make me blest.

2 Thou great and good, thou just and wise,
Thou art my Father and my God;
And I am thine by sacred ties;
Thy son, thy servant bought with blood.

3 With heart, and eyes and lifted hands,
For thee I long, to thee I look,
As travellers in thirsty lands
Pant for the cooling water-brook.

4 With early feet I love t' appear
Among thy saints and seek thy face;
Oft have I seen thy glory there,
And felt the power of sovereign grace.

5 Not fruits nor wines that tempt our taste,
Not all the joys our senses know,
Could make me so divinely blest
Or raise my cheerful passions so.

6 My life itself without thy love
No taste of pleasure could afford;
'Twould but a tiresome burden prove,
If I were banish'd from the Lord.

7 Amidst the wakeful hours of night,
When busy cares afflict my head
One thought of thee gives new delight,
And adds refreshment to my bed.

8 I'll lift my hands, I'll raise my voice,
While I have breath to pray or praise;
This work shall make my heart rejoice,
And spend the remnant of my days.

Psalm 63:4. S. M.
Seeking God.

1 My God, permit my tongue
This joy, to call thee mine,
And let my early cries prevail
To taste thy love divine.

2 My thirsty fainting soul
Thy mercy doth implore;
Not travellers in desert lands
Can pant for water more.

3 Within thy churches, Lord,
I long to find my place,
Thy power and glory to behold,
And feel thy quickening grace.

4 For life without thy love
No relish can afford;
No joy can be compar'd to this,
To serve and please the Lord.

5 To thee I'll lift my hands,
And praise thee while I live;
Not the rich dainties of a feast
Such food or pleasure give.

6 In wakeful hours at night
I call my God to mind;
I think how wise thy counsels are,
And all thy dealings kind.

7 Since thou hast been my help,
To thee my spirit flies,
And on thy watchful providence
My cheerful hope relies.

8 The shadow of thy wings
My soul in safety keeps;
I follow where my Father leads,
And he supports my steps.

Psalm 65:1. 1-5. First Part. L. M.
Public prayer and praise.

1 The praise of Sion waits for thee,
My God; and praise becomes thy house;
There shall thy saints thy glory see,
And there perform their public vows.

2 O thou, whose mercy bends the skies
To save when humble sinners pray,
All lands to thee shall lift their eyes
And islands of the northern sea.

3 Against my will my sins prevail,
But grace shall purge away their stain;

The blood of Christ will never fail
To wash my garments white again.

4 Blest is the man whom thou shalt choose,
And give him kind access to thee,
Give him a place within thy house,
To taste thy love divinely free.

PAUSE.

5 Let Babel fear when Sion prays;
Babel, prepare for long distress
When Sion's God himself arrays
In terror, and in righteousness.

6 With dreadful glory God fulfils
What his afflicted saints request;
And with almighty wrath reveals
His love to give his churches rest.

7 Then shall the flocking nations run
To Sion's hill, and own their Lord;
The rising and the setting sun
Shall see their Saviour's name ador'd.

Psalm 65:2. 5-13. Second Part. L. M. Divine
providence in air, earth, and sea; or, The God of
nature and grace.

1 The God of our salvation hears
The groans of Sion mix'd with tears;
Yet when he comes with kind designs,
Thro' all the way his terror shines.

2 On him the race of man depends,
Far as the earth's remotest ends,
Where the Creator's Name is known
By nature's feeble light alone.

3 Sailors, that travel o'er the flood,
Address their frighted souls to God;
When tempests rage and billows roar
At dreadful distance from the shore.

4 He bids the noisy tempest cease;
He calms the raging crowd to peace,
When a tumultuous nation raves
Wild as the winds, and loud as waves.

5 Whole kingdoms shaken by the storm
He settles in a peaceful form;
Mountains establish'd by his hand,
Firm on their old foundations stand.

6 Behold his ensigns sweep the sky,
New comets blaze and lightnings fly,
The heathen lands, with swift surprise,
From the bright horrors turn their eyes.

7 At his command the morning-ray
Smiles in the east, and leads the day;
He guides the sun's declining wheels
Over the tops of western hills.

8 Seasons and times obey his voice;
The evening and the morn rejoice
To see the earth made soft with showers,
Laden with fruit and drest in flowers.

9 'Tis from his watery stores on high
He gives the thirsty ground supply;
He walks upon the clouds, and thence
Doth his enriching drops dispense.

10 The desert grows a fruitful field,
Abundant food the vallies yield;
The vallies shout with cheerful voice,
And neighb'ring hills repeat their joys.

11 The pastures smile in green array;
There lambs and larger cattle play;
The larger cattle and the lamb
Each in his language speaks thy Name.

12 Thy works pronounce thy power divine,
O'er every field thy glories shine;
Thro' every month thy gifts appear;
Great God! thy goodness crowns the year.

Psalm 65:3. First Part. C. M.
A prayer-hearing God, and the Gentiles called.

1 Praise waits in Sion, Lord, for thee;
There shall our vows be paid:
Thou hast an ear when sinners pray,
All flesh shall seek thine aid.

2 Lord, our iniquities prevail,
But pardoning grace is thine,

And thou wilt grant us power and skill
To conquer every sin.

3 Bless'd are the men whom thou wilt choose
To bring them near thy face,
Give them a dwelling in thine house
To feast upon thy grace.

4 In answering what thy church requests
Thy truth and terror shine,
And works of dreadful righteousness
Fulfil thy kind design.

5 Thus shall the wondering nations see
The Lord is good and just;
And distant islands fly to thee,
And make thy Name their trust.

6 They dread thy glittering tokens, Lord,
When signs in heaven appear;
But they shall learn thy holy word,
And love as well as fear.

Psalm 65:4. Second Part. C. M. The providence
of God in air, earth, and sea; or, The blessing of
rain.

1 'Tis by thy strength the mountains stand,
God of eternal power;
The sea grows calm at thy command,
And tempests cease to roar.

2 Thy morning light and evening shade
Successive comforts bring;
Thy plenteous fruits make harvest glad,
Thy flowers adorn the spring.

3 Seasons and times, and moons and hours,
Heaven, earth, and air are thine;
When clouds distil in fruitful showers,
The author is divine.

4 Those wandering cisterns in the sky,
Borne by the winds around,
With watery treasures well supply
The furrows of the ground.

5 The thirsty ridges drink their fill,
And ranks of corn appear;

Thy ways abound with blessings still,
Thy goodness crowns the year.

Psalm 65:5. Third Part. C. M. The blessing: of
the spring; or, God gives rain. A psalm for the
husbandman.

1 Good is the Lord, the heavenly King,
Who makes the earth his care,
Visits the pastures every spring,
And bids the grass appear.

2 The clouds, like rivers rais'd on high,
Pour out, at thy command,
Their watery blessings from the sky,
To cheer the thirsty land.

3 The soften'd ridges of the field
Permit the corn to spring;
The vallies rich provision yield,
And the poor labourers sing.

4 The little hills on every side
Rejoice at falling showers;
The meadows, drest in all their pride,
Perfume the air with flowers.

5 The barren clods, refresh'd with rain,
Promise a joyful crop;
The parching grounds look green again,
And raise the reaper's hope.

6 The various months thy goodness crowns;
How bounteous are thy ways;
The bleating flocks spread o'er the downs,
And shepherds shout thy praise.

Psalm 66:1. First Part. Governing power and
goodness; or, Our graces tried by afflictions.

1 Sing, all ye nations, to the Lord,
Sing with a joyful noise;
With melody of sound record
His honours, and your joys.

2 Say to the power that shakes the sky,
"How terrible art thou!
"Sinners before thy presence fly,
"Or at thy feet they bow."

3 [Come, see the wonders of our God,
How glorious are his ways:
In Moses' hand he puts his rod,
And cleaves the frighted seas.

4 He made the ebbing channel dry,
While Israel pass'd the flood;
There did the church begin their joy,
And triumph in their God.]

5 He rules by his resistless might:
Will rebel mortals dare
Provoke th' Eternal to the fight,
And tempt that dreadful war?

6 O bless our God and never cease;
Ye saints, fulfil his praise;
He keeps our life, maintains our peace,
And guides our doubtful ways.

7 Lord, thou hast prov'd our suffering souls,
To make our graces shine;
So silver bears the burning coals
The metal to refine.

8 Thro' watery deeps and fiery ways
We march at thy command,
Led to possess the promis'd place
By thine unerring hand.

Psalm 66:2. 13-20. Second Part.
Praise to God for hearing prayer.

1 Now shall my solemn vows be paid
To that Almighty power,
That heard the long requests I made
In my distressful hour.

2 My lips and cheerful heart prepare
To make his mercies known;
Come, ye that fear my God, and hear
The wonders he has done.

3 When on my head huge sorrows fell,
I sought his heavenly aid,
He sav'd my sinking soul from hell,
And death's eternal shade.

4 If sin lay cover'd in my heart,
While prayer employ'd my tongue,

The Lord had shewn me no regard,
Nor I his praises sung.

5 But God, (his Name be ever blest)
Hath set my spirit free,
Nor turn'd from him my poor request,
Nor turn'd his heart from me.

Psalm 67.
The nation's prosperity and the church's
increase.

1 Shine, mighty God, on Britain shine
With beams of heavenly grace;
Reveal thy power thro' all our coasts,
And shew thy smiling face.

2 [Amidst our isle, exalted high,
Do thou our glory stand,
And like a wall of guardian fire
Surround the favourite land.]

3 When shall thy Name, from shore to shore,
Sound all the earth abroad,
And distant nations know and love
Their Saviour and their God?

4 Sing to the Lord, ye distant lands,
Sing loud with solemn voice;
While British tongues exalt his praise,
And British hearts rejoice.

5 He the great Lord, the sovereign Judge,
That sits enthron'd above,
Wisely commands the worlds he made
In justice and in love.

6 Earth shall obey her Maker's will,
And yield a full increase;
Our God will crown his chosen isle
With fruitfulness and peace.

7 God the Redeemer scatters round
His choicest favours here,
While the creation's utmost bound
Shall see, adore, and fear.

Psalm 68:1. 1-6 32-35. First Part.
The vengeance and compassion of God.

1 Let God arise in all his might,
And put the troops of hell to flight,
As smoke that sought to cloud the skies
Before the rising tempest flies.

2 [He comes array'd in burning flames;
Justice and vengeance are his names:
Behold his fainting foes expire
Like melting wax before the fire.]

3 He rides and thunders thro' the sky;
His name Jehovah sounds on high:
Sing to his Name, ye sons of grace;
Ye saints, rejoice before his face.

4 The widow and the fatherless
Fly to his aid in sharp distress;
In him the poor and helpless find
A Judge that's just, a Father kind.

5 He breaks the captive's heavy chain,
And prisoners see the light again;
But rebels that dispute his will,
Shall dwell in chains and darkness still.

PAUSE.

6 Kingdoms and thrones to God belong;
Crown him, ye nations, in your song;
His wondrous names and powers rehearse;
His honours shall enrich your verse.

7 He shakes the heavens with loud alarms;
How terrible is God in arms!
In Israel are his mercies known,
Israel is his peculiar throne.

8 Proclaim him King, pronounce him blest!
He's your defence, your joy, your rest:
When terrors rise and nations faint,
God is the strength of every saint.

Psalm 68:2. 17 18. Second Part.
Christ's ascension, and the gift of the Spirit.

1 Lord, when thou didst ascend on high,
Ten thousand angels fill'd the sky;

Those heavenly guards around thee wait,
Like chariots that attend thy state.

2 Not Sinai's mountain could appear
More glorious when the Lord was there;
While he pronounc'd his dreadful law,
And struck the chosen tribes with awe.

3 How bright the triumph none can tell,
When the rebellious powers of hell
That thousand souls had captive made,
Were all in chains like captives led.

4 Rais'd by his Father to the throne,
He sent the promis'd Spirit down,
With gifts and grace for rebel men,
That God might dwell on earth again.

Psalm 68:3. 19 9 20-2. Third Part.
Praise for temporal blessings; or,
Common and special mercies.

1 We bless the Lord, the just, the good,
Who fills our hearts with joy and food;
Who pours his blessings from the skies,
And loads our days with rich supplies.

2 He sends the sun his circuit round,
To cheer the fruits, to warm the ground;
He bids the clouds with plenteous rain
Refresh the thirsty earth again.

3 'Tis to his care we owe our breath,
And all our near escapes from death;
Safety and health to God belong;
He heals the weak, and guards the strong.

4 He makes the saint and sinner prove
The common blessings of his love;
But the wide difference that remains,
Is endless joy, or endless pains.

5 The Lord, that bruis'd the serpent's head,
On all the serpent's seed shall tread;
The stubborn sinner's hope confound,
And smite him with a lasting wound.

6 But his right hand his saints shall raise
From the deep earth, or deeper seas,

And bring them to his courts above,
There shall they taste his special love.

Psalm 69:1. 1-14. First Part. C. M.
The sufferings of Christ for our salvation.

1 "Save me, O God, the swelling floods
"Break in upon my soul:
"I sink, and sorrows o'er my head
"Like mighty waters roll.

2 "I cry till all my voice be gone,
"In tears I waste the day:
"My God behold my longing eyes,
"And shorten thy delay.

3 "They hate my soul without a cause,
"And still their number grows
"More than the hairs around my head,
"And mighty are my foes.

4 "'Twas then I paid that dreadful debt
"That men could never pay,
"And gave those honours to thy law
"Which sinners took away."

5 Thus in the great Messiah's name,
The royal prophet mourns;
Thus he awakes our hearts to grief,
And gives us joy by turns.

6 "Now shall the saints rejoice and find
"Salvation in my Name:
"For I have borne their heavy load
Of sorrow, pain, and shame.

7 "Grief, like a garment, cloth'd me round,
"And sackcloth was my dress,
"While I procur'd for naked souls
"A robe of righteousness.

8 "Amongst my brethren and the Jews
"I like a stranger stood,
"And bore their vile reproach to bring
"The Gentiles near to God.

9 "I came in sinful mortals' stead,
"To do my Father's will;

"Yet when I cleans'd my father's house
"They scandaliz'd my zeal.

10 "My fasting and my holy groans
"Were made the drunkard's song;
"But God, from his celestial throne,
"Heard my complaining tongue.

11 "He sav'd me from the dreadful deep,
"Nor let my soul be drown'd;
"He rais'd and fix'd my sinking feet
"On well establish'd ground.

12 "'Twas in a most accepted hour
"My prayer arose on high,
"And for my sake my God shall hear
"The dying sinner's cry."

Psalm 69:2. 14-21 26 29 32. 2d Part. C. M.
The passion and exaltation of Christ.

1 Now let our lips with holy fear
And mournful pleasure sing
The sufferings of our great High-Priest,
The sorrows of our King.

2 He sinks in floods of deep distress:
How high the waters rise!
While to his heavenly Father's ear
He sends perpetual cries.

3 "Hear me, O Lord, and save thy Son,
"Nor hide thy shining face;
"Why should thy favorite look like one
"Forsaken of thy grace?

4 "With rage they persecute the man
"That groans beneath thy wound,
"While for a sacrifice I pour
"My life upon the ground.

5 "They tread my honour to the dust,
"And laugh when I complain
"Their sharp insulting slanders add
"Fresh anguish to my pain.

6 "All my reproach is known to thee,
"The scandal and the shame;
"Reproach has broke my bleeding heart,
"And lies defil'd my Name.

7 "I look'd for pity, but in vain;
"My kindred are my grief!
"I ask my friends for comfort round,
"But meet with no relief.

8 "With vinegar they mock my thirst;
"They give me gall for food;
"And sporting with my dying groans,
"They triumph in my blood.

9 "Shine into my distressed soul,
"Let thy compassion save;
"And tho' my flesh sink down to death,
"Redeem it from the grave.

10 "I shall arise to praise thy Name,
"Shall reign in worlds unknown;
"And thy salvation, O my God,
"Shall seat me on thy throne."

Psalm 69:3. Third Part. C. M.
Christ's obedience and death; or,
God glorified and sinners saved.

1 Father, I sing thy wondrous grace,
I bless my Saviour's Name,
He bought salvation for the poor,
And bore the sinner's shame.

2 His deep distress has rais'd us high,
His duty and his zeal
Fulfill'd the law which mortals broke,
And finish'd all thy will.

3 His dying groans, his living songs
Shall better please my God
Than harp or trumpet's solemn sound,
Than goats' or bullocks' blood.

4 This shall his humble followers see,
And set their hearts at rest;
They by his death draw near to thee,
And live for ever blest.

5 Let heaven, and all that dwell on high,
To God their voices raise,
While lands and seas assist the sky,
And join t' advance the praise.

6 Zion is thine, most holy God;
Thy Son shall bless her gates;
And glory purchas'd by his blood
For thine own Israel waits.

Psalm 69:4. First Part. L. M.
Christ's passion, and sinners' salvation.

1 Deep in our hearts let us record
The deeper sorrows of our Lord;
Behold the rising billows roll
To overwhelm his holy soul.

2 In long complaints he spends his breath,
While hosts of hell, and powers of death,
And all the sons of malice join
To execute their curst design.

3 Yet, gracious God, thy power and love
Has made the curse a blessing prove;
Those dreadful sufferings of thy Son
Aton'd for sins which we had done.

4 The pangs of our expiring Lord
The honours of thy law restor'd;
His sorrows made thy justice known,
And paid for follies not his own.

6 O for his sake our guilt forgive,
And let the mourning sinner live;
The Lord will hear us in his Name,
Nor shall our hope be turn'd to shame.

Psalm 69:5. 7 &c. Second Part. L. M.
Christ's sufferings and zeal.

1 'Twas for thy sake, eternal God,
Thy son sustain'd that heavy load
Of base reproach and sore disgrace,
And shame defil'd his sacred face.

2 The Jews, his brethren and his kin,
Abus'd the man that check'd their sin:
While he fulfill'd thy holy laws,
They hate him, but without a cause.

3 ["My Father's house, said he, was made
"A place for worship, not for trade;"

Then scattering all their gold and brass,
He scourg'd the merchants from the place.]

4 [Zeal for the temple of his God
Consum'd his life, expos'd his blood:
Reproaches at thy glory thrown
He felt, and mourn'd them as his own.]

5 [His friends forsook, his followers fled,
While foes and arms surround his head;
They curse him with a slanderous tongue,
And the false judge maintains the wrong.]

6 His life they load with hateful lies,
And charge his lips with blasphemies;
They nail him to the shameful tree:
There hung the man that dy'd for me.

7 [Wretches with hearts as hard as stones,
Insult his piety and groans;
Gall was the food they gave him there,
And mock'd his thirst with vinegar.]

8 But God beheld; and from his throne
Marks out the men that hate his Son;
The hand that rais'd him from the dead
Shall pour the vengeance on their head.

Psalm 71:1. 5-9. First Part.
The aged saint's reflection and hope.

1 My God, my everlasting hope,
I live upon thy truth;
Thine hands have held my childhood up,
And strengthen'd all my youth.

2 My flesh was fashion'd by thy power,
With all these limbs of mine;
And from my mother's painful hour
I've been entirely thine.

3 Still has my life new wonders seen
Repeated every year;
Behold my days that yet remain,
I trust them to thy care.

4 Cast me not off when strength declines,
When hoary hairs arise;
And round me let thy glories shine
Whene'er thy servant dies.

5 Then in the history of my age,
When men review my days,
They'll read thy love in every page,
In every line thy praise.

Psalm 71:2. 15 14 16 23 22 24. 2d Part.
Christ our strength and righteousness.

1 My Saviour, my almighty Friend,
When I begin thy praise,
Where will the growing numbers end,
The numbers of thy grace?

2 Thou art my everlasting trust,
Thy goodness I adore;
And since I knew thy graces first
I speak thy glories more.

3 My feet shall travel all the length
Of the celestial road,
And march with courage in thy strength
To see my Father God.

4 When I am fill'd with sore distress
For some surprising sin,
I'll plead thy perfect righteousness,
And mention none but thine.

5 How will my lips rejoice to tell
The victories of my King!
My soul redeem'd from sin and hell
Shall thy salvation sing.

6 [My tongue shall all the day proclaim
My Saviour and my God;
His death has brought my foes to shame,
And drown'd them in his blood.

7 Awake, awake my tuneful powers;
With this delightful song
I'll entertain the darkest hours,
Nor think the season long.]

Psalm 71:3. 17-21. Third Part.
The aged Christian's prayer and song; or,
Old age, death, and the resurrection.

1 God of my childhood and my youth,
The guide of all my days,

I have declar'd thy heavenly truth,
And told thy wondrous ways.

2 Wilt thou forsake my hoary hairs,
And leave my fainting heart?
Who shall sustain my sinking years
If God my strength depart?

3 Let me thy power and truth proclaim
To the surviving age,
And leave a savour of thy Name
When I shall quit the stage.

4 The land of silence and of death
Attends my next remove;
O may these poor remains of breath
Teach the wide world thy love.

PAUSE.

5 Thy righteousness is deep and high,
Unsearchable thy deeds;
Thy glory spreads beyond the sky,
And all my praise exceeds.

6 Oft have I heard thy threatenings roar,
And oft endur'd the grief;
But when thy hand has press'd me sore,
Thy grace was my relief.

7 By long experience have I known
Thy sovereign power to save;
At thy command I venture down
Securely to the grave.

8 When I lie buried deep in dust,
My flesh shall be thy care
These withering limbs with thee I trust
To raise them strong and fair.

Psalm 72:1. First Part.
The kingdom of Christ.

1 Great God, whose universal sway
The known and unknown worlds obey,
Now give the kingdom to thy Son,
Extend his power, exalt his throne.

2 Thy sceptre well becomes his hands,
All heaven submits to his commands;

His justice shall avenge the poor,
And pride and rage prevail no more.

3 With power he vindicates the just,
And treads th' oppressor in the dust;
His worship and his fear shall last
Till hours and years and time be past.

4 As rain on meadows newly mown
So shall he send his influence down;
His grace on fainting souls distils
Like heavenly dew on thirsty hills.

5 The heathen lands that lie beneath
The shades of overspreading death,
Revive at his first dawning light,
And deserts blossom at the sight.

6 The saints shall flourish in his days,
Drest in the robes of joy and praise;
Peace like a river from his throne
Shall flow to nations yet unknown.

Psalm 72:2. Second Part.
Christ's kingdom among the Gentiles.

1 Jesus shall reign where'er the sun
Does his successive journies run;
His kingdom stretch from shore to shore,
Till moons shall wax and wane no more.

2 [Behold the islands with their kings,
And Europe her best tribute brings;
From north to south the princes meet
To pay their homage at his feet.

3 There Persia glorious to behold,
There India shines in eastern gold:
And barbarous nations at his word
Submit, and bow, and own their Lord.]

4 For him shall endless prayer be made
And princes throng to crown his head;
His Name like sweet perfume shall rise
With every morning sacrifice.

5 People and realms of every tongue
Dwell on his love with sweetest song:
And infant voices shall proclaim
Their early blessings on his Name.

6 Blessings abound where'er he reigns,
The prisoner leaps to lose his chains,
The weary find eternal rest,
And all the sons of want are blest.

7 [Where he displays his healing power,
Death and the curse are known no more;
In him the tribes of Adam boast
More blessings than their father lost.

8 Let every creature rise, and bring
Peculiar honours to our King;
Angels descend with songs again,
And earth repeat the long Amen.]

Psalm 73:1. First Part. C. M. Afflicted saints
happy, and prosperous sinners cursed.

1 Now I'm convinc'd the Lord is kind
To men of heart sincere,
Yet once my foolish thoughts repin'd
And border'd on despair.

2 I griev'd to see the wicked thrive,
And spoke with angry breath,
"How pleasant and profane they live!
"How peaceful is their death!

3 "With well-fed flesh and haughty eyes
"They lay their fears to sleep;
"Against the heavens their slanders rise,
"While saints in silence weep.

4 "In vain I lift my hands to pray,
"And cleanse my heart in vain,
"For I am chasten'd all the day,
"The night renews my pain.'

5 Yet while my tongue indulg'd complaints,
I felt my heart reprove;
"Sure I shall thus offend thy saints,
"And grieve the men I love."

6 But still I found my doubts too hard,
The conflict too severe,
Till I retir'd to search thy word,
And learn thy secrets there.

7 There, as in some prophetic glass,
I saw the sinner's feet

High mounted on a slippery place,
Beside a fiery pit.

8 I heard the wretch profanely boast,
Till at thy frown he fell;
His honours in a dream were lost,
And he awakes in hell.

9 Lord, what an envious fool I was!
How like a thoughtless beast!
Thus to suspect thy promis'd grace,
And think the wicked blest.

10 Yet I was kept from full despair,
Upheld by power unknown;
That blessed hand that broke the snare
Shall guide me to thy throne.

Psalm 73:2. 23-8. Second Part.
God our portion here and hereafter.

1 God my supporter and my hope,
My help for ever near,
Thine arm of mercy held me up
When sinking in despair.

2 Thy counsels, Lord, shall guide my feet
Thro' this dark wilderness;
Thine hand conduct me near thy seat
To dwell before thy face.

3 Were I in heaven without my God,
'Twould be no joy to me;
And whilst this earth is my abode,
I long for none but thee.

4 What if the springs of life were broke,
And flesh and heart should faint!
God is my soul's eternal rock,
The strength of every saint.

5 Behold the sinners that remove
Far from thy presence die;
Not all the idol gods they love
Can save them when they cry.

6 But to draw near to thee, my God,
Shall be my sweet employ;
My tongue shall sound thy works abroad,
And tell the world my joy.

Psalm 73:3. 22 3 6 17-20. L. M.
The prosperity of sinners cursed.

1 Lord, what a thoughtless wretch was I,
To mourn, and murmur, and repine
To see the wicked plac'd on high,
In pride and robes of honour shine!

2 But O their end, their dreadful end!
Thy sanctuary taught me so:
On slippery rocks I see them stand,
And fiery billows roll below.

3 Now let them boast how tall they rise,
I'll never envy them again;
There they may stand with haughty eyes,
Till they plunge deep in endless pain.

4 Their fancy'd joys, how fast they flee!
Just like a dream when man awakes;
Their songs of softest harmony
Are but a preface to their plagues.

5 Now I esteem their mirth and wine
Too dear to purchase with my blood;
Lord, 'tis enough that thou art mine,
My life, my portion, and my God.

Psalm 73:4. S. M.
The mystery of providence unfolded.

1 Sure there's a righteous God,
Nor is religion vain,
Tho' men of vice may boast aloud,
And men of grace complain.

2 I saw the wicked rise,
And felt my heart repine,
While haughty fools with scornful eyes
In robes of honour shine.

3 [Pamper'd with wanton ease,
Their flesh looks full and fair,
Their wealth rolls in like flowing seas,
And grows without their care.

4 Free from the plagues and pains
That pious souls endure,
Thro' all their life oppression reigns
And racks the humble poor.

5 Their impious tongues blaspheme
The everlasting God;
Their malice blasts the good man's name,
And spreads their lies abroad.

6 But I with flowing tears
Indulge my doubts to rise
"Is there a God that sees or hears
"The things below the skies?"]

7 The tumults of my thought
Held me in hard suspense,
Till to thy house my feet were brought
To learn thy justice thence.

8 Thy word with light and power
Did my mistakes attend;
I view'd the sinners' life before,
But here I learnt their end.

9 On what a slippery steep
The thoughtless wretches go;
And O that dreadful fiery deep
That waits their fall below.

10 Lord, at thy feet I bow,
My thoughts no more repine;
I call my God my portion now,
And all my powers are thine.

Psalm 74. The church pleading with God under sore persecutions.

1 Will God for ever cast us off?
His wrath for ever smoke
Against the people of his love,
His little chosen flock?

2 Think of the tribes so dearly bought
With their Redeemer's blood;
Nor let thy Sion be forgot,
Where once thy glory stood.

3 Lift up thy feet and march in haste,
Aloud our ruin calls;
See what a wide and fearful waste
Is made within thy walls.

4 Where once thy churches pray'd and sang
Thy foes profanely roar;

Over thy gates their ensigns hang,
Sad tokens of their power.

5 How are the seats of worship broke!
They tear the buildings down,
And he that deals the heaviest stroke
Procures the chief renown.

6 With flames they threaten to destroy
Thy children in their nest;
"Come let us burn at once (they cry)
The temple and the priest."

7 And still to heighten our distress
Thy presence is withdrawn;
Thy wonted signs of power and grace,
Thy power and grace are gone.

8 No prophet speaks to calm our woes,
But all the seers mourn;
There's not a soul amongst us knows
The time of thy return.

PAUSE.

9 How long, eternal God, how long
Shall men of pride blaspheme?
Shall saints be made their endless song,
And bear immortal shame?

10 Canst thou for ever sit and hear
Thine holy Name profan'd?
And still thy jealousy forbear,
And still withhold thine hand?

11 What strange deliverance hast thou shown
In ages long before!
And now no other God we own,
No other God adore.

12 Thou didst divide the raging sea
By thy resistless might,
To make thy tribes a wondrous way,
And then secure their flight.

13 Is not the world of nature thine,
The darkness and the day?
Didst thou not bid the morning shine,
And mark the sun his way?

14 Hath not thy power form'd every coast,
And set the earth its bounds,
With summer's heat and winter's frost,
In their perpetual rounds?

15 And shall the sons of earth and dust
That sacred power blaspheme?
Will not thy hand that form'd them first
Avenge thine injur'd Name?

16 Think on the covenant thou hast made,
And all thy words of love;
Nor let the birds of prey invade
And vex thy mourning dove.

17 Our foes would triumph in our blood,
And make our hope their jest;
Plead thy own cause, almighty God!
And give thy children rest.

Psalm 75.
Power and government from God alone.
Applied to the glorious Revolution by King
William, or
the happy Accession of King George to the
Throne.

1 To thee, most holy, and most high,
To thee, we bring our thankful praise;
Thy works declare thy name is nigh,
Thy works of wonder and of grace.

2 Britain was doom'd to be a slave,
Her frame dissolv'd, her fears were great;
When God a new supporter gave
To bear the pillars of the state.

3 He from thy hand receiv'd his crown,
And sware to rule by wholesome laws
His foot shall tread th' oppressor down,
His arm defend the righteous cause.

4 Let haughty sinners sink their pride,
Nor lift so high their scornful head;
But lay their foolish thoughts aside,
And own the king that God hath made.

5 Such honours never come by chance,
Nor do the winds promotion blow;

'Tis God the judge doth one advance,
'Tis God that lays another low.

6 No vain pretence to royal birth
Shall fix a tyrant on the throne:
God the great sovereign of the earth
Will rise and make his justice known.

7 [His hand holds out the dreadful cup
Of vengeance, mix'd with various plagues,
To make the wicked drink them up,
Wring out and taste the bitter dregs.

8 Now shall the Lord exalt the just,
And while he tramples on the proud,
And lays their glory in the dust,
My lips shall sing his praise aloud.]

Psalm 76. Israel saved, and the Assyrians
destroyed; or, God's vengeance against his
enemies proceeds from his church.

1 In Judah God of old was known;
His Name in Israel great;
In Salem stood his holy throne,
And Sion was his seat.

2 Among the praises of his saints
His dwelling there he chose;
There he receiv'd their just complaints
Against their haughty foes.

3 From Sion went his dreadful word,
And broke the threatening spear;
The bow, the arrows, and the sword,
And crush'd th' Assyrian war.

4 What are the earth's wide kingdoms else
But mighty hills of prey?
The hill on which Jehovah dwells
Is glorious more than they.

5 'Twas Sion's King that stopt the breath
Of captains and their bands:
The men of might slept fast in death,
And never found their hands.

6 At thy rebuke, O Jacob's God,
Both horse and chariot fell;

Who knows the terrors of thy rod?
Thy vengeance who can tell?

7 What power can stand before thy sight
When once thy wrath appears?
When heaven shines round with dreadful light,
The earth lies still and fears.

8 When God in his own sovereign ways
Comes down to save th' opprest,
The wrath of man shall work his praise,
And he'll restrain the rest.

9 [Vow to the Lord, and tribute bring,
Ye princes, fear his frown:
His terror shakes the proudest king,
And cuts an army down.

10 The thunder of his sharp rebuke
Our haughty foes shall feel:
For Jacob's God hath not forsook,
But dwells in Sion still.]

Psalm 77:1. First Part.
Melancholy assaulting, and hope prevailing.

1 To God I cry'd with mournful voice,
I sought his gracious ear,
In the sad day when troubles rose,
And fill'd the night with fear.

2 Sad were my days, and dark my nights,
My soul refus'd relief;
I thought on God the just and wise,
But thoughts increas'd my grief.

3 Still I complain'd, and still opprest,
My heart began to break;
My God, thy wrath forbid my rest,
And kept my eyes awake.

4 My overwhelming sorrows grew
Till I could speak no more;
Then I within myself withdrew,
And call'd thy judgments o'er.

5 I call'd back years and ancient times,
When I beheld thy face;
My spirit search'd for secret crimes
That might withhold thy grace.

6 I call'd thy mercies to my mind
Which I enjoy'd before;
And will the Lord no more be kind?
His face appear no more?

7 Will he for ever cast me off?
His promise ever fail?
Has he forgot his tender love?
Shall anger still prevail?

8 But I forbid this hopeless thought,
This dark despairing frame,
Rememb'ring what thy hand hath wrought,
Thy hand is still the same.

9 I'll think again of all thy ways,
And talk thy wonders o'er;
Thy wonders of recovering grace,
When flesh could hope no more.

10 Grace dwells with justice on the throne;
And men that love thy word
Have in thy sanctuary known
The counsels of the Lord.

Psalm 77:2. Second Part.
Comfort derived from ancient providences; or,
Israel delivered from Egypt, and brought to
Canaan.

1 "How awful is thy chastening rod!"
(May thine own children say)
"The great, the wise, the dreadful God!
"How holy is his way!"

2 I'll meditate his works of old;
The King that reigns above;
I'll hear his ancient wonders told,
And learn to trust his love.

3 Long did the house of Joseph lie
With Egypt's yoke opprest:
Long he delay'd to hear their cry,
Nor gave his people rest.

4 The sons of good old Jacob seem'd
Abandon'd to their foes;
But his almighty arm redeem'd
The nation that he chose.

5 Israel, his people, and his sheep,
Must follow where he calls;
He bid them venture thro' the deep,
And made the waves their walls.

6 The waters saw thee, mighty God!
The waters saw thee come;
Backward they fled, and frighted stood,
To make thine armies room.

7 Strange was thy journey thro' the sea,
Thy footsteps, Lord, unknown,
Terrors attend the wondrous way
That brings thy mercies down.

8 [Thy voice with terror in the sound
Thro' clouds and darkness broke;
All heaven in lightning shone around,
And earth with thunder shook.

9 Thine arrows thro' the skies were hurl'd;
How glorious is the Lord!
Surprise and trembling seiz'd the world,
And his own saints ador'd.

10 He gave them water from the rock;
And safe by Moses' hand
Thro' a dry desert led his flock
Home to the promis'd land.]

Psalm 78:1. First Part. Providence of God
recorded; or, Pious education and instruction of
children.

1 Let children hear the mighty deeds,
Which God perform'd of old,
Which in our younger years we saw,
And which our fathers told.

2 He bids us make his glories known,
His works of power and grace;
And we'll convey his wonders down
Thro' every rising race.

3 Our lips shall tell them to our Sons,
And they again to theirs,
That generations yet unborn
May teach them to their heirs.

4 Thus shall they learn in God alone
Their hope securely stands,
That they may ne'er forget his works,
But practise his commands.

Psalm 78:2. Second Part. Israel's rebellion and
punishment; or, The sins and chastisements of
God's people.

1 What a stiff rebellious house
Was Jacob's ancient race!
False to their own most solemn vows,
And to their Maker's grace.

2 They broke the covenant of his love,
And did his laws despise,
Forgot the works he wrought to prove
His power before their eyes.

3 They saw the plagues on Egypt light,
From his revenging hand:
What dreadful tokens of his might
Spread o'er the stubborn land!

4 They saw him cleave the mighty sea,
And march'd in safety thro',
With watery walls to guard their way,
Till they had 'scap'd the foe.

5 A wondrous pillar mark'd the road,
Compos'd of shade and light;
By day it prov'd a sheltering cloud,
A leading fire by night.

6 He from the rock their thirst supply'd;
The gushing waters fell,
And ran in rivers by their side,
A constant miracle.

7 Yet they provok'd the Lord most high,
And dar'd distrust his hand;
"Can he with bread our host supply
"Amidst this desert land?"

8 The Lord with indignation heard,
And caus'd his wrath to flame
His terrors ever stand prepar'd
To vindicate his Name.

Psalm 78:3. Third Part. The punishment of luxury and intemperance; or, Chastisement and salvation.

1 When Israel sins, the Lord reproves,
And fills their hearts with dread;
Yet he forgives the men he loves,
And sends them heavenly bread.

2 He fed them with a liberal hand,
And made his treasures known;
He gave the midnight clouds command
To pour provision down.

3 The manna, like a morning shower,
Lay thick around their feet;
The corn of heaven, so light, so pure,
As tho' 'twere angels' meat.

4 But they in murmuring language said,
"Manna is all our feast;
"We loathe this light, this airy bread;
"We must have flesh to taste."

5 "Ye shall have flesh to please your lust;"
The Lord in wrath reply'd,
And sent them quails like sand or dust,
Heap'd up from side to side.

6 He gave them all their own desire;
And greedy as they fed,
His vengeance burnt with secret fire,
And smote the rebels dead.

7 When some were slain, the rest return'd,
And sought the Lord with tears;
Under the rod they fear'd and mourn'd,
But soon forgot their fears.

8 Oft he chastis'd and still forgave,
Till by his gracious hand
The nation he resolv'd to save,
Possess'd the promis'd land.

Psalm 78:4. 32 &c. Fourth Part.
Backsliding and forgiveness; or,
Sin punished, and saints saved.

1 Great God, how oft did Israel prove
By turns thine anger and thy love!

There in a glass our hearts may see
How fickle and how false they be.

2 How soon the faithless Jews forgot
The dreadful wonders God had wrought!
Then they provoke him to his face,
Nor fear his power, nor trust his grace.

3 The Lord consum'd their years in pain,
And made their travels long and vain;
A tedious march thro' unknown ways
Wore out their strength and spent their days.

4 Oft when they saw their brethren slain,
They mourn'd and sought the Lord again;
Call'd him the Rock of their abode,
Their high Redeemer and their God.

5 Their prayers and vows before him rise
As flattering words or solemn lies,
While their rebellious tempers prove
False to his covenant and his love.

6 Yet did his sovereign grace forgive
The men who not deserv'd to live;
His anger oft away he turn'd,
Or else with gentle flame it burn'd.

7 He saw their flesh was weak and frail,
He saw temptation still prevail
The God of Abraham lov'd them still,
And led them to his holy hill.

Psalm 80. The church's prayer under affliction; or, The vineyard of God wasted.

1 Great Shepherd of thine Israel,
Who didst between the cherubs dwell,
And led the tribes, thy chosen sheep,
Safe thro' the desert and the deep.

2 Thy church is in the desert now,
Shine from on high and guide us thro';
Turn us to thee, thy love restore,
We shall be sav'd, and sigh no more.

3 Great God, whom heavenly hosts obey,
How long shall we lament and pray,
And wait in vain thy kind return?
How long shall thy fierce anger burn?

4 Instead of wine and cheerful bread,
Thy saints with their own tears are fed;
Turn us to thee, thy love restore,
We shall be sav'd, and sigh no more.

PAUSE I.

5 Hast thou not planted with thy hands
A lovely vine in heathen lands?
Did not thy power defend it round,
And heavenly dews enrich the ground?

6 How did the spreading branches shoot,
And bless the nations with the fruit!
But now, dear Lord, look down and see
Thy mourning vine, that lovely tree.

7 Why is its beauty thus defac'd?
Why hast thou laid her fences waste?
Strangers and foes against her join,
And every beast devours the vine.

8 Return, almighty God, return,
Nor let thy bleeding vineyard mourn;
Turn us to thee, thy love restore,
We shall be sav'd, and sigh no more.

PAUSE II.

9 Lord, when this vine in Canaan grew
Thou wast its strength and glory too;
Attack'd in vain by all its foes,
Till the fair Branch of Promise rose;

10 Fair Branch, ordain'd of old to shoot
From David's stock, from Jacob's root;
Himself a noble vine, and we
The lesser branches of the tree.

11 'Tis thy own Son, and he shall stand
Girt with thy strength at thy right hand;
Thy first-born Son, adorn'd and blest
With power and grace above the rest.

12 O! for his sake attend our cry,
Shine on thy churches lest they die;
Turn us to thee, thy love restore,
We shall be sav'd, and sigh no more.

Psalm 81. 1 8 16.
The warnings of God to his people; or,
Spiritual blessings and punishments.

1 Sing to the Lord aloud,
And make a joyful noise;
God is our strength, our Saviour God;
Let Israel hear his voice.

2 "From vile idolatry
"Preserve my worship clean;
"I am the Lord who set thee free
"From slavery and sin.

3 "Stretch thy desires abroad,
"And I'll supply them well
"But if ye will refuse your God,
"If Israel will rebel,

4 "I'll leave them," saith the Lord,
"To their own lusts a prey,
"And let them run the dangerous road,
"'Tis their own chosen way.

5 "Yet O! that all my saints
"Would hearken to my voice!
"Soon I would ease their sore complaints,
"And bid their hearts rejoice.

6 "While I destroy their foes,
"I'd richly feed my flock,
"And they should taste the stream that flows
"From their eternal Rock."

Psalm 82. God the supreme Governor; or,
Magistrates warned.

1 Among th' assemblies of the great,
A greater Ruler takes his seat;
The God of heaven, as Judge, surveys
Those gods on earth and all their ways.

2 Why will ye then frame wicked laws?
Or why support th' unrighteous cause?
When will ye once defend the poor,
That sinners vex the saints no more?

3 They know not, Lord, nor will they know,
Dark are the ways in which they go;

Their name of earthly gods is vain,
For they shall fall and die like men.

4 Arise, O Lord, and let thy Son
Possess his universal throne,
And rule the nations with his rod;
He is our judge, and he our God.

Psalm 83.
A complaint against persecutors.

1 And will the God of grace
Perpetual silence keep?
The God of justice hold his peace,
And let his vengeance sleep?

2 Behold what cursed snares
The men of mischief spread;
The men that hate thy saints and thee
Lift up their threatening head.

3 Against thy hidden ones
Their counsels they employ,
And malice with her watchful eye,
Pursues them to destroy.

4 The noble and the base
Into thy pastures leap;
The lion and the stupid ass
Conspire to vex thy sheep.

5 "Come, let us join," they cry,
"To root them from the ground,
"Till not the name of saints remain,
"Nor memory shall be found."

6 Awake, almighty God,
And call thy wrath to mind;
Give them like forests to the fire,
Or stubble to the wind.

7 Convince their madness, Lord,
And make them seek thy Name
Or else their stubborn rage confound,
That they may die in shame.

8 Then shall the nations know
That glorious dreadful word,
Jehovah is thy name alone,
And thou the sovereign Lord.

Psalm 84:1. First Part. L. M.
The pleasure of public worship.

1 How pleasant, how divinely fair,
O Lord of hosts, thy dwellings are!
With long desire my spirit faints
To meet th' assemblies of thy saints.

2 My flesh would rest in thine abode,
My panting heart cries out for God;
My God! my King! why should I be
So far from all my joys and thee?

3 The sparrow chuses where to rest,
And for her young provides her nest:
But will my God to sparrows grant
That pleasure which his children want?

4 Blest are the saints who sit on high,
Around thy throne of majesty;
Thy brightest glories shine above,
And all their work is praise and love.

5 Blest are the souls that find a place
Within the temple of thy grace;
There they behold thy gentler rays,
And seek thy face, and learn thy praise.

6 Blest are the men whose hearts are set
To find the way to Sion's gate;
God is their strength, and thro' the road
They lean upon their helper God.

7 Cheerful they walk with growing strength,
Till all shall meet in heaven at length,
Till all before thy face appear,
And join in nobler worship there.

Psalm 84:2. Second Part. L. M.
God and his church; or, Grace and glory.

1 Great God, attend, while Sion sings
The joy that from thy presence springs
To spend one day with thee on earth
Exceeds a thousand days of mirth.

2 Might I enjoy the meanest place
Within thine house, O God of grace,
Not tents of ease, nor thrones of power,
Should tempt my feet to leave thy door.

3 God is our sun, he makes our day;
God is our shield, he guards our way
From all th' assaults of hell and sin,
From foes without, and foes within.

4 All needful grace will God bestow,
And crown that grace with glory too:
He gives us all things, and withholds
No real good from upright souls.

5 O God, our King, whose sovereign sway
The glorious hosts of heaven obey,
And devils at thy presence flee,
Blest is the man that trusts in thee.

Psalm 84:3. 14 2 3 10. Paraphrased. C. M.
Delight in ordinances of worship; or, God
present in his churches.

1 My soul, how lovely is the place
To which thy God resorts!
'Tis heaven to see his smiling face,
Tho' in his earthly courts.

2 There the great Monarch of the skies
His saving power displays,
And light breaks in upon our eyes
With kind and quickening rays.

3 With his rich gifts the heavenly Dove
Descends and fills the place,
While Christ reveals his wondrous love,
And sheds abroad his grace.

4 There, mighty God, thy words declare
The secrets of thy will;
And still we seek thy mercy there,
And sing thy praises still.

PAUSE.

5 My heart and flesh cry out for thee,
While far from thine abode:
When shall I tread thy courts, and see
My Saviour and my God?

6 The sparrow builds herself a nest,
And suffers no remove;
O make me like the sparrows, blest,
To dwell but where I love.

7 To sit one day beneath thine eye,
And hear thy gracious voice,
Exceeds a whole eternity
Employ'd in carnal joys.

8 Lord, at thy threshold I would wait,
While Jesus is within,
Rather than fill a throne of state,
Or live in tents of sin.

9 Could I command the spacious land,
And the more boundless sea,
For one blest hour at thy right hand
I'd give them both away.

Psalm 84:4. As the 148th Psalm.
Longing for the house of God.

1 Lord of the worlds above,
How pleasant and how fair
The dwellings of thy love,
Thy earthly temples are!
To thine abode
My heart aspires,
With warm desires
To see my God.

2 The sparrow, for her young,
With pleasure seeks her nest;
And wandering swallows long
To find their wonted rest:
My spirit faints
With equal zeal
To rise and dwell
Among thy saints.

3 O happy souls that pray
Where God appoints to hear!
O happy men that pay
Their constant service there!
They praise thee still;
And happy they
That love the way
To Zion's hill.

4 They go from strength to strength,
Thro' this dark vale of tears,
Till each arrives at length,
Till each in heaven appears:
O glorious seat,

When God our king
Shall thither bring
Our willing feet!

PAUSE.

5 To spend one sacred day
Where God and saints abide,
Affords diviner joy
Than thousand days beside;
Where God resorts,
I love it more
To keep the door
Than shine in courts.

6 God is our sun and shield,
Our light and our defence
With gifts his hands are fill'd,
We draw our blessings thence;
He shall bestow
On Jacob's race
Peculiar grace
And glory too.

7 The Lord his people loves;
His hand no good withholds
From those his heart approves,
From pure and pious souls:
Thrice happy he,
O God of hosts,
Whose spirit trusts
Alone in thee.

Psalm 85:1. 1-8. First Part.
Waiting for an answer to prayer; or,
Deliverance begun and completed.

1 Lord, thou hast call'd thy grace to mind,
Thou hast revers'd our heavy doom:
So God forgave when Israel sinn'd,
And brought his wandering captives home.

2 Thou hast begun to set us free,
And made thy fiercest wrath abate;
Now let our hearts be turn'd to thee,
And thy salvation be complete.

3 Revive our dying graces, Lord,
And let thy saints in thee rejoice;

Make known thy truth, fulfil thy word,
We wait for praise to tune our voice.

4 We wait to hear what God will say;
He'll speak, and give his people peace;
But let them run no more astray,
Lest his returning wrath increase.

Psalm 85:2. 9 &c. Second Part.
Salvation by Christ.

1 Salvation is for ever nigh
The souls that fear and trust the Lord;
And grace descending from on high,
Fresh hopes of glory shall afford.

2 Mercy and truth on earth are met,
Since Christ the Lord came down from heaven;
By his obedience, so complete,
Justice is pleas'd, and peace is given.

3 Now truth and honour shall abound,
Religion dwell on earth again,
And heavenly influence bless the ground
In our Redeemer's gentle reign.

4 His righteousness is gone before
To give us free access to God;
Our wandering feet shall stray no more,
But mark his steps and keep the road.

Psalm 86. 8-13.
A general song of praise to God.

1 Among the princes, earthly gods,
There's none hath power divine;
Nor is their nature, mighty Lord,
Nor are their works like thine.

2 The nations thou hast made shall bring
Their offerings round thy throne;
For thou alone dost wondrous things,
For thou art God alone.

3 Lord, I would walk with holy feet;
Teach me thine heavenly ways,
And my poor scatter'd thoughts unite
In God my Father's praise.

4 Great is thy mercy, and my tongue
Shall those sweet wonders tell,
How by thy grace my sinking soul
Rose from the deeps of hell.

Psalm 87.
The church the birth-place of the saints; or,
Jews and Gentiles united in the Christian
Church.

1 God in his earthly temple lays
Foundations for his heavenly praise:
He likes the tents of Jacob well,
But still in Zion loves to dwell.

2 His mercy visits every house
That pay their night and morning vows;
But makes a more delightful stay
Where churches meet to praise and pray.

3 What glories were describ'd of old!
What wonders are of Zion told!
Thou city of our God below,
Thy fame shall Tyre and Egypt know.

4 Egypt and Tyre, and Greek and Jew,
Shall there begin their lives anew:
Angels and men shall join to sing
The hill where living waters spring.

5. When God makes up his last account
Of natives in his holy mount,
'Twill be an honour to appear
As one new-born or nourish'd there.

Psalm 89:1. First Part. L. M.
The covenant made with Christ; or, the true
David.

1 For ever shall my song record
The truth and mercy of the Lord;
Mercy and truth for ever stand,
Like heaven, establish'd by his hand.

2 Thus to his Son he sware, and said,
"With thee my covenant first is made;
"In thee shall dying sinners live,
"Glory and grace are thine to give.

3 "Be thou my prophet, thou my priest;
"Thy children shall be ever blest;
"Thou art my chosen king; thy throne
"Shall stand eternal like my own.

4 "There's none of all my sons above,
"So much my image or my love;
"Celestial powers thy subjects are,
"Then what can earth to thee compare?

5 "David, my servant, whom I chose
"To guard my flock, to crush my foes,
"And rais'd him to the Jewish throne,
"Was but a shadow of my Son."

6 Now let the church rejoice and sing
Jesus her Saviour and her King:
Angels his heavenly wonders show,
And saints declare his works below.

Psalm 89:2. First Part. C. M.
The faithfulness of God.

1 My never-ceasing songs shall show
The mercies of the Lord,
And make succeeding ages know
How faithful is his word.

2 The sacred truths his lips pronounce
Shall firm as heaven endure;
And if he speak a promise once,
Th' eternal grace is sure.

3 How long the race of David held
The promis'd Jewish throne!
But there's a nobler covenant seal'd
To David's greater Son.

4 His seed for ever shall possess
A throne above the skies;
The meanest subject of his grace
Shall to that glory rise.

5 Lord God of hosts, thy wondrous ways
Are sung by saints above;
And saints on earth their honours raise
To thine unchanging love.

Psalm 89:3. 7 &c. Second Part. The power and majesty of God; or, Reverential worship.

1 With reverence let the saints appear
And bow before the Lord,
His high commands with reverence hear,
And tremble at his word.

2 How terrible thy glories be!
How bright thine armies shine!
Where is the power that vies with thee?
Or truth compar'd to thine?

3 The northern pole and southern rest
On thy supporting hand;
Darkness and day from east to west
Move round at thy command.

4 Thy words the raging wind control,
And rule the boisterous deep;
Thou mak'st the sleeping billows roll,
The rolling billows sleep.

5 Heaven, earth, and air, and sea are thine,
And the dark world of hell:
How did thine arm in vengeance shine
When Egypt durst rebel!

6 Justice and judgment are thy throne,
Yet wondrous is thy grace;
While truth and mercy join'd in one
Invite us near thy face.

Psalm 89:4. 15 &c. Third Part.
A blessed gospel.

1 Blest are the souls that hear and know
The gospel's joyful sound;
Peace shall attend the path they go,
And light their steps surround.

2 Their joy shall bear their spirits up
Thro' their Redeemer's Name;
His righteousness exalts their hope,
Nor Satan dares condemn.

3 The Lord, our glory and defence,
Strength and salvation gives;
Israel, thy king for ever reigns,
Thy God for ever lives.

Psalm 89:5. 19 &c. Fourth Part.
Christ's mediatorial kingdom; or,
His divine and human nature.

1 Hear what the Lord in vision said,
And made his mercy known:
"Sinners, behold your help is laid
"On my almighty Son.

2 "Behold the man my wisdom chose
"Among your mortal race;
"His head my holy oil o'erflows,
"The Spirit of my grace.

3 "High shall he reign on David's throne,
"My people's better King;
"My arm shall beat his rivals down,
"And still new subjects bring.

4 "My truth shall guard him in his way,
"With mercy by his side,
"While, in my name thro' earth and sea
"He shall in triumph ride.

5 "Me for his Father and his God
"He shall for ever own,
"Call me his rock, his high abode;
"And I'll support my Son.

6 "My first-born Son array'd in grace
"At my right-hand shall sit;
"Beneath him angels know their place,
"And monarchs at his feet.

7 "My covenant stands for ever fast,
"My promises are strong;
"Firm as the heavens his throne shall last,
"His seed endure as long."

Psalm 89:6. 30 &c. Fifth Part. The covenant of grace unchangeable; or, Afflictions without rejection.

1 "Yet (saith the Lord) if David's race,
"The children of my Son,
"Should break my laws, abuse my grace,
"And tempt mine anger down;

2 "Their sins I'll visit with the rod,
"And make their folly smart;

"But I'll not cease to be their God,
"Nor from my truth depart.

3 "My covenant I will ne'er revoke,
"But keep my grace in mind;
"And what eternal love hath spoke
"Eternal truth shall bind.

4 "Once have I sworn (I need no more)
"And pledg'd my holiness
"To seal the sacred promise sure
"To David and his race.

5 "The sun shall see his offspring rise
"And spread from sea to sea,
"Long as he travels round the skies
"To give the nations day.

6 "Sure as the moon that rules the night
"His kingdom shall endure,
"Till the fix'd laws of shade and light
"Shall be observ'd no more."

Psalm 89:7. 47 &c. Sixth Part.
Mortality and hope.
A funeral psalm.

1 Remember, Lord, our mortal state,
How frail our life, how short the date!
Where is the man that draws his breath
Safe from disease, secure from death?

2 Lord, while we see whole nations die,
Our flesh and sense repine and cry,
"Must death for ever rage and reign?
"Or hast thou made mankind in vain?

3 "Where is thy promise to the just?
"Are not thy servants turn'd to dust?"
But faith forbids these mournful sighs,
And sees the sleeping dust arise.

4 That glorious hour, that dreadful day
Wipes the reproach of saints away,
And clears the honour of thy word;
Awake our souls, and bless the Lord.

Psalm 89:8. 47 &c. Last Part.
As the 113th Psalm.
Life, death, and the resurrection.

1 Think, mighty God, on feeble man,
How few his hours, how short his span!
Short from the cradle to the grave:
Who can secure his vital breath
Against the bold demands of death,
With skill to fly, or power to save?

2 Lord, shall it be for ever said,
"The race of man was only made
"For sickness, sorrow, and the dust?"
Are not thy servants day by day
Sent to their graves, and turn'd to clay?
Lord, where's thy kindness to the just?

3 Hast thou not promis'd to thy Son
And all his seed a heavenly crown?
But flesh and sense indulge despair;
For ever blessed be the Lord,
That faith can read his holy word,
And find a resurrection there.

4 For ever blessed be the Lord,
Who gives his saints a long reward
For all their toil, reproach and pain;
Let all below and all above
Join to proclaim thy wondrous love,
And each repeat their loud Amen.

Psalm 90:1. L. M.
Man mortal, and God eternal.
A mournful song at a funeral.

1 Thro' every age, eternal God,
Thou art our rest, our safe abode;
High was thy throne ere heaven was made,
Or earth thy humble footstool laid.

2 Long hadst thou reign'd ere time began,
Or dust was fashion'd to a man;
And long thy kingdom shall endure
When earth and time shall be no more.

3 But man, weak man, is born to die,
Made up of guilt and vanity;
Thy dreadful sentence, Lord, was just,
"Return, ye sinners, to your dust."

4 [A thousand of our years amount
Scarce to a day in thine account;
Like yesterday's departed light,
Or the last watch of ending night.]

PAUSE.

5 Death like an overflowing stream
Sweeps us away; our life's a dream;
An empty tale; a morning flower
Cut down and wither'd in an hour.

6 [Our age to seventy years is set;
How short the term! how frail the state!
And if to eighty we arrive,
We rather sigh and groan than live.

7 But O how oft thy wrath appears,
And cuts off our expected years!
Thy wrath awakes our humble dread;
We fear the power that strikes us dead.]

8 Teach us, O Lord, how frail is man;
And kindly lengthen out our span,
Till a wise care of piety
Fit us to die, and dwell with thee.

Psalm 90:2. 1-5. First Part. C. M.
Man frail, and God eternal.

1 Our God, our help in ages past,
Our hope for years to come,
Our shelter from the stormy blast,
And our eternal home.

2 Under the shadow of thy throne
Thy saints have dwelt secure;
Sufficient is thine arm alone,
And our defence is sure.

3 Before the hills in order stood,
Or earth receiv'd her frame,
From everlasting thou art God,
To endless years the same.

4 Thy word commands our flesh to dust,
"Return, ye sons of men:"
All nations rose from earth at first,
And turn to earth again.

5 A thousand ages in thy sight
Arc like an evening gone;
Short as the watch that ends the night
Before the rising sun.

6 [The busy tribes of flesh and blood,
With all their lives and cares,
Are carried downwards by thy flood,
And lost in following years.

7 Time like an ever-rolling stream
Bears all its Sons away;
They fly forgotten as a dream
Dies at the opening day.

8 Like flowery fields the nations stand
Pleas'd with the morning light;
The flowers beneath the mower's hand
Lie withering ere 'tis night.]

9 Our God, our help in ages past,
Our hope for years to come,
Be thou our guard while troubles last,
And our eternal home.

Psalm 90:3. 8 11 9 10 12. 2d Part. C. M.
Infirmities and mortality the effect of sin; or,
Life, old age, and preparation for death.

1 Lord, if thine eyes survey our faults,
And justice grow severe,
Thy dreadful wrath exceeds our thoughts,
And burns beyond our fear.

2 Thine anger turns our frame to dust;
By one offence to thee
Adam with all his sons have lost
Their immortality.

3 Life like a vain amusement flies,
A fable or a song;
By swift degrees our nature dies,
Nor can our joys be long.

4 'Tis but a few whose days amount To
threescore years and ten, And all beyond that
short account is sorrow, toil, and pain.

5 [Our vitals with laborious strife
Bear up the crazy load,

And drag those poor remains of life
Along the tiresome road.]

6 Almighty God, reveal thy love,
And not thy wrath alone;
O let our sweet experience prove
The mercies of thy throne!

7 Our souls would learn the heavenly art
T' improve the hours we have,
That we may act the wiser part,
And live beyond the grave.

Psalm 90:4. 13 &c. Third Part. C. M.
Breathing after heaven.

1 Return, O God of love, return;
Earth is a tiresome place:
How long shall we thy children mourn
Our absence from thy face!

2 Let heaven succeed our painful years,
Let sin and sorrow cease,
And in proportion to our tears
So make our joys increase.

3 Thy wonders to thy servants show,
Make thy own work complete,
Then shall our souls thy glory know,
And own thy love was great.

4 Then shall we shine before thy throne
In all thy beauty, Lord;
And the poor service we have done
Meet a divine reward.

Psalm 90:5. 5 10 12. S. M.
The frailty and shortness of life.

1 Lord what a feeble piece
Is this our mortal frame!
Our life how poor a trifle 'tis,
That scarce deserves the name!

2 Alas the brittle clay
That built our body first!
And every month, and every day
'Tis mouldering back to dust.

3 Our moments fly apace,
Nor will our minutes stay;
Just like a flood our hasty days
Are sweeping us away.

4 Well if our days must fly,
We'll keep their end in sight,
We'll spend them all in wisdom's way,
And let them speed their flight.

5 They'll waft us sooner o'er
This life's tempestuous sea:
Soon we shall reach the peaceful shore
Of blest eternity.

Psalm 91:1. 1-7. First Part.
Safety in public diseases and dangers.

1 He that hath made his refuge God,
Shall find a most secure abode,
Shall walk all day beneath his shade,
And there at night shall rest his head.

2 Then will I say, "My God, thy power
"Shall be my fortress and my tower;
"I that am form'd of feeble dust
"Make thine almighty arm my trust."

3 Thrice happy man! thy Maker's care
Shall keep thee from the fowler's snare,
Satan, the fowler, who betrays
Unguarded souls a thousand ways.

4 Just as a hen protects her brood
From birds of prey that seek their blood,
Under her feathers, so the Lord
Makes his own arm his people's guard.

5 If burning beams of noon conspire
To dart a pestilential fire,
God is their life; his wings are spread
To shield them with an healthful shade.

6 If vapours with malignant breath
Rise thick and scatter midnight death,
Israel is safe; the poison'd air
Grows pure if Israel's God be there.

PAUSE.

7 What though a thousand at thy side,
At thy right hand ten thousand dy'd,
Thy God his chosen people saves
Amongst the dead, amidst the graves.

8 So when he sent his angel down
To make his wrath in Egypt known,
And slew their sons, his careful eye
Pass'd all the doors of Jacob by.

9 But if the fire, or plague, or sword,
Receive commission from the Lord
To strike his saints among the rest,
Their very pains and deaths are blest.

10 The sword, the pestilence or fire
Shall but fulfil their best desire,
From sins and sorrows set them free,
And bring thy children, Lord, to thee.

Psalm 91:2. 1-16. Second Part. Protection from
death, guard of angels, victory and deliverance.

1 Ye sons of men, a feeble race,
Expos'd to every snare,
Come make the Lord your dwelling-place,
And try and trust his care.

2 No ill shall enter where you dwell;
Or if the plague come nigh,
And sweep the wicked down to hell,
'Twill raise his saints on high.

3 He'll give his angels charge to keep
Your feet in all their ways;
To watch your pillow while you sleep,
And guard your happy days.

4 Their hands shall bear you, lest you fall
And dash against the stones:
Are they not servants at his call,
And sent t' attend his sons?

5 Adders and lions ye shall tread;
The tempter's wiles defeat;
He that hath broke the serpent's head
Puts him beneath your feet.

6 "Because on me they set their love
"I'll save them," saith the Lord;

"I'll bear their joyful souls above
"Destruction and the sword.

7 "My grace shall answer when they call;
"In trouble I'll be nigh;
"My power shall help them when they fall,
"And raise them when they die.

8 "Those that on earth my Name have known,
"I'll honour them in heaven;
"There my salvation shall be shown,
"And endless life be given."

Psalm 92:1. First Part.
A psalm for the Lord's day.

1 Sweet is the work, my God my King,
To praise thy Name, give thanks and sing,
To shew thy love by morning light,
And talk of all thy truth at night.

2 Sweet is the day of sacred rest,
No mortal cares shall seize my breast;
O may my heart in tune be found
Like David's harp of solemn sound!

3 My heart shall triumph in my Lord,
And bless his works, and bless his word;
Thy works of grace, how bright they shine!
How deep thy counsels! how divine!

4 Fools never raise their thoughts so high;
Like brutes they live, like brutes they die;
Like grass they flourish, till thy breath
Blast them in everlasting death.

5 But I shall share a glorious part
When grace hath well refin'd my heart,
And fresh supplies of joy are shed
Like holy oil, to cheer my head.

6 Sin, (my worst enemy before)
Shall vex my eyes and ears no more;
My inward foes shall all be slain,
Nor Satan break my peace again.

7 Then shall I see, and hear, and know,
All I desir'd or wish'd below;
And every power find sweet employ
In that eternal world of joy.

Psalm 92:2. 12 &c. Second Part.
The church is the garden of God.

1 Lord, 'tis a pleasant thing to stand
In gardens planted by thine hand;
Let me within thy courts be seen
Like a young cedar fresh and green.

2 There grow thy saints in faith and love,
Blest with thine influence from above;
Not Lebanon with all its trees
Yields such a comely sight as these.

3 The plants of grace shall ever live;
(Nature decays but grace must thrive)
Time, that doth all things else impair,
Still makes them flourish strong and fair.

4 Laden with fruits of age, they shew
The Lord is holy, just, and true;
None that attend his gates shall find
A God unfaithful or unkind.

Psalm 93:1. 1st Metre. As 100th Psalm.
The eternal and sovereign God.

1 Jehovah reigns; he dwells in light,
Girded with majesty and might:
The world created by his hands
Still on its first foundation stands.

2 But ere this spacious world was made,
Or had its first foundations laid,
Thy throne eternal ages stood,
Thyself the ever-living God.

3 Like floods the angry nations rise
And aim their rage against the skies;
Vain floods that aim their rage so high!
At thy rebuke the billows die.

4 For ever shall thy throne endure;
Thy promise stands for ever sure;
And everlasting holiness
Becomes the dwellings of thy grace.

Psalm 93:2. 2d M. As the old 50th Psalm.
The same.

1 The Lord of glory reigns; he reigns on high;
His robes of state are strength and majesty:
This wide creation rose at his command,
Built by his word, and 'stablish'd by his hand:
Long stood his throne ere he began creation,
And his own Godhead is the firm foundation.

2 God is th' eternal King: thy foes in vain
Raise their rebellions to confound thy reign:
In vain the storms, in vain the floods arise,
And roar and toss their waves against the skies;
Foaming at heaven, they rage with wild commotion,
But heaven's high arches scorn the swelling ocean.

3 Ye tempests, rage no more; ye floods, be still;
And the mad world submissive to his will:
Built on his truth, his church must ever stand;
Firm are his promises, and strong his hand:
See his own sons, when they appear before him,
Bow at his footstool, and with fear adore him.

Psalm 93:3. 3d M. As the old 122d Psalm.
The same.

1 The Lord Jehovah reigns
And royal state maintains,
His head with awful glories crown'd;
Array'd in robes of light,
Begirt with sovereign might,
And rays of majesty around.

2 Upheld by thy commands
The world securely stands;
And skies and stars obey thy word:
Thy throne was fix'd on high
Before the starry sky;
Eternal is thy kingdom, Lord.

3 In vain the noisy crowd,
Like billows fierce and loud,
Against thine empire rage and roar;
In vain, with angry spite,
The surly nations fight,
And dash like waves against the shore.

4 Let floods and nations rage,
And all their powers engage,
Let swelling tides assault the sky;

The terrors of thy frown
Shall beat their madness down;
Thy throne for ever stands on high.

5 Thy promises are true,
Thy grace is ever new;
There fix'd thy church shall ne'er remove:
Thy saints with holy fear
Shall in thy courts appear,
And sing thine everlasting love.

Repeat the fourth stanza to complete the old
tune.

Psalm 94:1. 1 2 7-14. First Part. Saints
chastised, and sinners destroyed; or, Instructive
afflictions.

1 God, to whom revenge belongs,
Proclaim thy truth aloud
Let Sovereign Power redress our wrongs,
Let justice smite the proud.

2 They say, "The Lord nor sees nor hears;"
When will the fools be wise!
Can he be deaf who form'd their ears?
Or blind, who made their eyes?

3 He knows their impious thoughts are vain,
And they shall feel his power;
His wrath shall pierce their souls with pain
In some surprising hour.

4 But if thy saints deserve rebuke,
Thou hast a gentler rod;
Thy providences and thy book
Shall make them know their God.

5 Blest is the man thy hands chastise,
And to his duty draw;
Thy scourges make thy children wise
When they forget thy law.

6 But God will ne'er cast off his saints,
Nor his own promise break;
He pardons his inheritance
For their Redeemer's sake.

Psalm 94:2. 16-23. Second Part. God our
support and comfort; or, Deliverance from
temptation and persecution.

1 Who will arise and plead my right
Against my numerous foes,
While earth and hell their force unite,
And all my hopes oppose?

2 Had not the Lord, my rock, my help,
Sustain'd my fainting head,
My life had now in silence dwelt,
My soul amongst the dead.

3 "Alas! my sliding feet," I cry'd;
Thy promise was my prop;
Thy grace stood constant by my side,
Thy Spirit bore me up.

4 While multitudes of mournful thoughts
Within my bosom roll,
Thy boundless love forgives my faults,
Thy comforts cheer my soul.

5 Powers of iniquity may rise,
And frame pernicious laws;
But God, my refuge, rules the skies,
He will defend my cause.

6 Let malice vent her rage aloud,
Let bold blasphemers scoff;
The Lord our God shall judge the proud,
And cut the sinners off.

Psalm 95:1. C. M.
A psalm before prayer.

1 Sing to the Lord Jehovah's Name,
And in his strength rejoice;
When his salvation is our theme,
Exalted be our voice.

2 With thanks approach his awful sight,
And psalms of honour sing;
The Lord's a God of boundless might,
The whole creation's King.

3 Let princes hear, let angels know,
How mean their natures seem,

Those gods on high, and gods below,
When once compar'd with him.

4 Earth with its caverns dark and deep
Lies in his spacious hand,
He fix'd the seas what bounds to keep,
And where the hills must stand.

5 Come, and with humble souls adore,
Come, kneel before his face;
O may the creatures of his power
Be children of his grace!

6 Now is the time: he bends his ear,
And waits for your request;
Come, lest he rouse his wrath and swear
"Ye shall not see my rest."

Psalm 95:2. S. M.
A psalm before sermon.

1 Come, sound his praise abroad,
And hymns of glory sing;
Jehovah is the sovereign God,
The universal King.

He form'd the deeps unknown;
He gave the seas their bound;
The watery worlds are all his own,
And all the solid ground.

3 Come, worship at his throne,
Come bow before the Lord:
We are his works and not our own;
He form'd us by his word.

4 To-day attend his voice,
Nor dare provoke his rod;
Come like the people of his choice,
And own your gracious God.

5 But if your ears refuse
The language of his grace,
And hearts grow hard, like stubborn Jews,
That unbelieving race;

6 The Lord in vengeance drest
Will lift his hand and swear,
"You that despise my promis'd rest,
"Shall have no portion there."

Psalm 95:3. 1 2 3 6-11. L. M.
Canaan lost through unbelief; or,
A warning to delaying sinners.

1 Come, let our voices join to raise
A sacred song of solemn praise;
God is a sovereign King; rehearse
his honours in exalted verse.

2 Come, let our souls address the Lord,
Who fram'd our natures with his word;
He is our Shepherd; we the sheep
His mercy chose, his pastures keep.

3 Come, let us hear his voice to-day,
The counsels of his love obey;
Nor let our harden'd hearts renew
The sins and plagues that Israel knew.

4 Israel, that saw his works of grace,
Yet tempt their Maker to his face;
A faithless unbelieving brood
That tir'd the patience of their God.

5 Thus saith the Lord, "how false they prove;
"Forget my power, abuse my love;
"Since they despise my rest, I swear,
"Their feet shall never enter there."

6 [Look back my soul, with holy dread,
And view those ancient rebels dead;
Attend the offer'd grace to-day,
Nor lose the blessing by delay.

7 Seize the kind promise while it waits,
And march to Zion's heavenly gates;
Believe, and take the promis'd rest;
Obey, and be for ever blest.]

Psalm 96:1. 1-10. &c. C. M.
Christ's first and second coming.

1 Sing to the Lord, ye distant lands,
Ye tribes of every tongue;
His new discover'd grace demands
A new and nobler song.

2 Say to the nations, Jesus reigns,
God's own almighty Son;

His power the sinking world sustains,
And grace surrounds his throne.

3 Let heaven proclaim the joyful day,
Joy thro' the earth be seen;
Let cities shine in bright array,
And fields in cheerful green.

4 Let an unusual joy surprise
The islands of the sea;
Ye mountains, sink, ye vallies, rise,
Prepare the Lord his way.

5 Behold he comes, he comes to bless
The nations as their God;
To shew the world his righteousness,
And send his truth abroad.

6 But when his voice shall raise the dead,
And bid the world draw near,
How will the guilty nations dread
To see their Judge appear!

Psalm 96:2. As the 113th Psalm.
The God of the Gentiles.

1 Let all the earth their voices raise
To sing the choicest psalm of praise,
To sing and bless Jehovah's name:
His glory let the heathens know,
His wonders to the nations show,
And all his saving works proclaim.

2 The heathens know thy glory, Lord;
The wondering nations read thy word,
In Britain is Jehovah known:
Our worship shall no more be paid
To gods which mortal hands have made;
Our Maker is our God alone.

3 He fram'd the globe, he built the sky,
He made the shining worlds on high,
And reigns complete in glory there:
His beams are majesty and light;
His beauties how divinely bright!
His temple how divinely fair!

4 Come the great day, the glorious hour,
When earth shall feel his saving power,
And barbarous nations fear his name;

Then shall the race of man confess
The beauty of his holiness,
And in his courts his grace proclaim.

Psalm 97:1. 1-5. First Part.
Christ reigning in heaven, and coming to judgment.

1 He reigns; the Lord, the Saviour reigns;
Praise him in evangelic strains;
Let the whole earth in songs rejoice,
And distant islands join their voice.

2 Deep are his counsels and unknown;
But grace and truth support his throne:
Tho' gloomy clouds his ways surround,
Justice is their eternal ground.

3 In robes of judgment, lo! he comes,
Shakes the wide earth, and cleaves the tombs;
Before him burns devouring fire,
The mountains melt, the seas retire.

4 His enemies, with sore dismay,
Fly from the sight, and shun the day;
Then lift your heads, ye saints, on high,
And sing, for your redemption's nigh.

Psalm 97:2. 6-9. Second Part.
Christ's incarnation.

1 The Lord is come, the heavens proclaim
His birth; the nations learn his Name;
An unknown star directs the road
Of eastern sages to their God.

2 All ye bright armies of the skies,
Go, worship where the Saviour lies:
Angels and kings before him bow,
Those gods on high, and gods below.

3 Let idols totter to the ground,
And their own worshippers confound;
But Judah shout, but Zion sing,
And earth confess her sovereign King.

Psalm 97:3. Third Part.
Grace and glory.

1 Th' Almighty reigns exalted high
O'er all the earth, o'er all the sky,
Tho' clouds and darkness veil his feet,
His dwelling is the mercy-seat.

2 O ye that love his holy Name,
Hate every work of sin and shame;
He guards the souls of all his friends,
And from the snares of hell defends.

3 Immortal light and joys unknown
Are for the saints in darkness sown;
Those glorious seeds shall spring and rise,
And the bright harvest bless our eyes.

4 Rejoice, ye righteous, and record
The sacred honours of the Lord;
None but the soul that feels his grace
Can triumph in his holiness.

Psalm 97:4. 1 3 5-7 11. C. M.
Christ's incarnation, and the last judgment.

1 Ye islands of the northern sea,
Rejoice, the Saviour reigns;
His word like fire, prepares his way,
And mountains melt to plains.

2 His presence sinks the proudest hills,
And makes the vallies rise
The humble soul enjoys his smiles,
The haughty sinner dies.

3 The heavens his rightful power proclaim
The idol-gods around
Fill their own worshippers with shame,
And totter to the ground.

4 Adoring angels at his birth
Make the Redeemer known;
Thus shall he come to judge the earth,
And angels guard his throne.

5 His foes shall tremble at his sight,
And hills and seas retire
His children take their unknown flight,
And leave the world in fire.

6 The seeds of joy and glory sown
For saints in darkness here

Shall rise and spring in worlds unknown,
And a rich harvest bear.

Psalm 98:1. First Part.
Praise for the gospel.

1 To our almighty Maker, God, New honours be
address'd; his great salvation shines abroad, And
makes the nations blest.

2 He spake the word to Abraham first,
His truth fulfils the grace:
The Gentiles make his Name their trust,
And learn his righteousness.

3 Let the whole earth his love proclaim
With all her different tongues;
And spread the honours of his Name
In melody and songs.

Psalm 98:2. Second Part.
The Messiah's coming and kingdom.

1 Joy to the world; the Lord is come;
Let earth receive her King;
Let every heart prepare him room,
And heaven and nature sing.

2 Joy to the earth, the Saviour reigns;
Let men their songs employ;
While fields and floods, rocks, hills and plains,
Repeat the sounding joy.

3 No more let sins and sorrows grow,
Nor thorns infest the ground;
He comes to make his blessings flow
Far as the curse is found.

4 He rules the world with truth and grace,
And makes the nations prove
The glories of his righteousness,
And wonders of his love.

Psalm 99:1. First Part.
Christ's kingdom and majesty.

1 The God Jehovah reigns,
Let all the nations fear,

Let sinners tremble at his throne,
And saints be humble there.

2 Jesus the Saviour reigns,
Let earth adore its Lord;
Bright cherubs his attendants stand,
Swift to fulfil his word.

3 In Zion is his throne,
His honours are divine;
His church shall make his wonders known,
For there his glories shine.

4 How holy is his Name!
How terrible his praise!
Justice, and truth, and judgment join
In all his works of grace.

Psalm 99:2. Second Part.
A holy God worshipped with reverence.

1 Exalt the Lord our God,
And worship at his feet;
His nature is all holiness,
And mercy is his seat.

2 When Israel was his church,
When Aaron was his priest,
When Moses cry'd, when Samuel pray'd,
He gave his people rest.

3 Oft he forgave their sins,
Nor would destroy their race;
And oft he made his vengeance known,
When they abus'd his grace.

4 Exalt the Lord our God,
Whose grace is still time same;
Still he's a God of holiness,
And jealous for his Name.

Psalm 100:1. 1st M. A plain translation.
Praise to our Creator.

1 Ye nations round the earth rejoice
Before the Lord, your sovereign King;
Serve him with cheerful heart and voice,
With all your tongues his glory sing.

2 The Lord is God; 'tis he alone
Doth life, and breath, and being give:
We are his work, and not our own;
The sheep that on his pastures live.

3 Enter his gates with songs of joy,
With praises to his courts repair,
And make it your divine employ
To pay your thanks and honours there.

4 The Lord is good, the Lord is kind;
Great is his grace, his mercy sure;
And the whole race of man shall find
His truth from age to age endure.

Psalm 100:2. 2d M. A Paraphrase.

1 Sing to the Lord with joyful voice;
Let every land his name adore;
The British isles shall send the noise
Across the ocean to the shore.

2 Nations, attend before his throne
With solemn fear, with sacred joy;
Know that the Lord is God alone;
He can create, and he destroy.

3 His sovereign power, without our aid,
Made us of clay, and form'd us men;
And when like wandering sheep we stray'd,
He brought us to his fold again.

4 We are his people, we his care,
Our souls and all our mortal frame:
What lasting honours shall we rear,
Almighty Maker, to thy Name!

5 We'll crowd thy gates with thankful songs,
High as the heavens our voices raise;
And earth with her ten thousand tongues
Shall fill thy courts with sounding praise.

6 Wide as the world is thy command,
Vast as eternity thy love;
Firm as a rock thy truth must stand
When rolling years shall cease to move.

Psalm 101:1. L. M.
The Magistrate's psalm.

1 Mercy and judgment are my song;
And since they both to thee belong,
My gracious God, my righteous King,
To thee my songs and vows I bring.

2 If I am rais'd to bear the sword,
I'll take my counsels from thy word;
Thy justice and thy heavenly grace
Shall be the pattern of my ways.

3 Let wisdom all my actions guide,
And let my God with me reside;
No wicked thing shall dwell with me,
Which may provoke thy jealousy.

4 No sons of slander, rage and strife
Shall be companions of my life;
The haughty look, the heart of pride
Within my doors shall ne'er abide.

5 [I'll search the land, and raise the just
To posts of honour, wealth and trust:
The men that work thy holy will,
Shall be my friends and favourites still.]

6 In vain shall sinners hope to rise
By flattering or malicious lies;
And while the innocent I guard,
The bold offender shan't be spar'd.

7 The impious crew (that factious band)
Shall hide their heads, or quit the land;
And all that break the public rest,
Where I have power shall be supprest.

Psalm 101:2. C. M.
A psalm for a master of a family.

1 Of justice and of grace I sing,
And pay my God my vows;
Thy grace and justice, heavenly King,
Teach me to rule my house.

2 Now to my tent, O God, repair,
And make thy servant wise;
I'll suffer nothing near me there
That shall offend thine eyes.

3 The man that doth his neighbour wrong,
By falsehood or by force;
The scornful eye, the slanderous tongue,
I'll thrust them from my doors.

4 I'll seek the faithful and the just
And will their help enjoy;
These are the friends that I shall trust,
The servants I'll employ.

5 The wretch that deals in sly deceit,
I'll not endure a night;
The liar's tongue I ever hate,
And banish from my sight.

6 I'll purge my family around,
And make the wicked flee;
So shall my house be ever found
A dwelling fit for thee.

Psalm 102:1. 1-13 20 21. First Part.
A prayer of the afflicted.

1 Hear me, O God, nor hide thy face,
But answer lest I die;
Hast thou not built a throne of grace
To hear when sinners cry?

2 My days are wasted like the smoke
Dissolving in the air;
My strength is dry'd, my heart is broke,
And sinking in despair.

3 My spirits flag like withering grass
Burnt with excessive heat;
In secret groans my minutes pass,
And I forget to eat.

4 As on some lonely building's top
The sparrow tells her moan,
Far from the tents of joy and hope
I sit and grieve alone.

5 My soul is like a wilderness,
Where beasts of midnight howl;
There the sad raven finds her place,
And there the screaming owl.

6 Dark dismal thoughts and boding fears
Dwell in my troubled breast;

While sharp reproaches wound my ears,
Nor give my spirit rest.

7 My cup is mingled with my woes,
And tears are my repast;
My daily bread like ashes grows
Unpleasant to my taste.

8 Sense can afford no real joy
To souls that feel thy frown;
Lord, 'twas thy hand advanc'd me high,
Thy hand hath cast me down.

9 My looks like wither'd leaves appear,
And life's declining light
Grows faint as evening shadows are,
That vanish into night.

10 But thou for ever art the same,
O my eternal God:
Ages to come shall know thy Name,
And spread thy works abroad.

11 Thou wilt arise and shew thy face,
Nor will my Lord delay
Beyond th' appointed hour of grace,
That long expected day.

12 He hears his saints, he knows their cry,
And by mysterious ways
Redeems the prisoners doom'd to die,
And fills their tongues with praise.

Psalm 102:2. 13-21. Second Part.
Prayer heard and Zion restored.

1 Let Zion and her sons rejoice,
Behold the promis'd hour;
Her God hath heard her mourning voice,
And comes t' exalt his power.

2 Her dust and ruins that remain
Are precious in our eyes;
Those ruins shall be built again,
And all that dust shall rise.

3 The Lord will raise Jerusalem,
And stand in glory there;
Nations shall bow before has name,
And kings attend with fear.

4 He sits a sovereign on his throne,
With pity in his eyes;
He hears the dying prisoners groan,
And sees their sighs arise.

5 He frees the souls condemn'd to death,
And when his saints complain,
It shan't be said 'That praying breath
'Was ever spent in vain.'

6 This shall be known when we are dead,
And left on long record,
That ages yet unborn may read,
And trust, and praise the Lord.

Psalm 102:3. 25-28. Third Part.
Man's mortality and Christ's eternity; or,
Saints die, but Christ and the church live.

1 It is the Lord our Saviour's hand
Weakens our strength amidst the race;
Disease and death at his command
Arrest us, and cut short our days.

2 Spare us, O Lord, aloud we pray,
Nor let our sun go down at noon:
Thy years are one eternal day,
And must thy children die so soon?

3 Yet in the midst of death and grief
This thought our sorrow shall assuage,
"Our Father and our Saviour live;
"Christ is the same thro' every age."

4 'Twas he this earth's foundation laid;
Heaven is the building of his hand:
This earth grows old, these heavens shall fade,
And all be chang'd at his command.

5 The starry curtains of the sky
Like garments shall be laid aside;
But still thy throne stands firm and high;
Thy church for ever must abide.

6 Before thy face thy church shall live,
And on thy throne thy children reign;
This dying world shall they survive,
And the dead saints be rais'd again.

Psalm 103:1. 1-7. First Part. L. M.
Blessing God for his goodness to soul and body.

1 Bless, O my soul, the living God,
Call home thy thoughts that rove abroad;
Let all the powers within me join
In work and worship so divine.

2 Bless, O my soul, the God of grace;
His favours claim thy highest praise;
Why should the wonders he hath wrought
Be lost in silence and forgot?

3 'Tis he, my soul, that sent his Son
To die for crimes which thou hast done;
He owns the ransom; and forgives
The hourly follies of our lives.

4 The vices of the mind he heals,
And cures the pains that nature feels;
Redeems the soul from hell, and saves
Our wasting life from threat'ning graves.

5 Our youth decay'd his power repairs;
His mercy crowns our growing years;
He satisfies our mouth with good,
And fills our hopes with heavenly food.

6 He sees th' oppressor and th' opprest,
And often gives the sufferers rest;
But will his justice more display
In the last great rewarding day.

7 [His power he shew'd by Moses' hands,
And gave to Israel his commands;
But sent his truth and mercy down
To all the nations by his Son.

8 Let the whole earth his power confess,
Let the whole earth adore his grace;
The Gentile with the Jew shall join
In work and worship so divine.]

Psalm 103:2. 8-18. Second Part. L. M.
God's gentle chastisement; or,
His tender mercy to his people.

1. The Lord, how wondrous are his ways:
How firm his truth how large his grace;

He takes his mercy for his throne,
And thence he makes his glories known.

2 Not half so high his power hath spread
The starry heavens above our head,
As his rich love exceeds our praise,
Exceeds the highest hopes we raise.

3 Not half so far hath nature plac'd
The rising morning from the west,
As his forgiving grace removes
The daily guilt of those he loves.

4 How slowly doth his wrath arise!
On swifter wings salvation flies;
And if he lets his anger burn,
How soon his frowns to pity turn!

5 Amidst his wrath compassion shines;
His strokes are lighter than our sins;
And while his rod corrects his saints,
His ear indulges their complaints.

6 So fathers their young sons chastise,
With gentle hand and melting eyes;
The children weep beneath the smart,
And move the pity of their heart.

PAUSE.

7 The mighty God, the wise, and just,
Knows that our frame is feeble dust;
And will no heavy loads impose
Beyond the strength that he bestows.

8 He knows how soon our nature dies,
Blasted by every wind that flies;
Like grass we spring, and die as soon,
Or morning flowers that fade at noon.

9 But his eternal love is sure
To all the saints, and shall endure:
From age to age his truth shall reign,
Nor children's children hope in vain.

Psalm 103:3. 1-7. First Part, S. M.
Praise for spiritual and temporal mercies.

1 O Bless the Lord, my soul;
Let all within me join,

And aid my tongue to bless his Name,
Whose favours are divine.

2 O bless the Lord, my soul;
Nor let his mercies lie
Forgotten in unthankfulness,
And without praises die.

3 'Tis he forgives thy sins,
'Tis he relieves thy pain,
'Tis he that heals thy sicknesses,
And makes thee young again.

4 He crowns thy life with love,
When ransom'd from the grave;
He that redeem'd my soul from hell
Hath sovereign power to save.

5 He fills the poor with good;
He gives the sufferers rest;
The Lord hath judgments for the proud,
And justice for th' opprest.

6 His wondrous works and ways
He made by Moses known;
But sent the world his truth and grace
By his beloved Son.

Psalm 103:4. 8-18. Second Part. S. M.
Abounding compassion of God; or,
Mercy in the midst of judgment.

1 My soul, repeat his praise
Whose mercies are so great,
Whose anger is so slow to rise,
So ready to abate.

2 God will not always chide;
And when his strokes are felt,
His strokes are fewer than our crimes,
And lighter than our guilt.

3 High as the heavens are rais'd
Above the ground we tread,
So far the riches of his grace
Our highest thoughts exceed.

4 His power subdues our sins;
And his forgiving love,

Far as the east is from the west,
Doth all our guilt remove.

5 The pity of the Lord
To those that fear his Name,
Is such as tender parents feel;
He knows our feeble frame.

6 He knows we are but dust,
Scatter'd with every breath;
His anger, like a rising wind,
Can send us swift to death.

7 Our days are as the grass,
Or like the morning flower;
If one sharp blast sweep o'er the field,
It withers in an hour.

8 But thy compassions, Lord,
To endless years endure;
And children's children ever find
Thy words of promise sure.

Psalm 103:5. 19-22. Third Part. S. M. God's
universal dominion; or, Angels praise the Lord.

1 The lord, the sovereign King,
Hath fix'd his throne on high;
O'er all the heavenly world he rules,
And all beneath the sky.

2 Ye angels great in might,
And swift to do his will,
Bless ye the Lord, whose voice ye hear,
Whose pleasure ye fulfil.

3 Let the bright hosts who wait
The orders of their King,
And guard his churches when they pray,
Join in the praise they sing.

4 While all his wondrous works,
Thro' his vast kingdoms shew
Their Maker's glory, thou, my soul,
Shalt sing his graces too.

Psalm 104.
The glory of God in creation and providence.

1 My soul, thy great Creator praise;
When cloth'd in his celestial rays
He in full Majesty appears,
And, like a robe, his glory wears.

Note, This psalm may be sung to the tune of the
old 112th or 127th
Psalm, by adding the two following lines to
every stanza, viz.

Great is the Lord; what tongue can frame
An equal honour to his Name?

Otherwise it must be sung as the 100th psalm.

2 The heavens are for his curtains spread,
Th' unfathom'd deep he makes his bed;
Clouds are his chariot, when he flies
On winged storms across the skies.

3 Angels, whom his own breath inspires,
His ministers are flaming fires;
And swift as thought their armies move
To bear his vengeance, or his love.

4 The world's foundations by his hand
Are pois'd, and shall for ever stand;
He binds the ocean in his chain,
Lest it should drown the earth again.

5 When earth was cover'd with the flood,
Which high above the mountains stood,
He thunder'd, and the ocean fled,
Confin'd to its appointed bed.

6 The swelling billows know their bound,
And in their channels walk their round;
Yet thence convey'd by secret veins,
They spring on hills, and drench the plains.

7 He bids the crystal fountains flow,
And cheer the vallies as they go;
Tame heifers there their thirst allay,
And for the stream wild asses bray.

8 From pleasant trees which shade the brink
The lark and linnet light to drink;
Their songs the lark and linnet raise;
And chide our silence in his praise.

PAUSE I.

9 God from his cloudy cistern, pours
On the parch'd earth enriching showers;
The grove, the garden, and the field
A thousand joyful blessings yield.

10 He makes the grassy food arise,
And gives the cattle large supplies;
With herbs for man of various power,
To nourish nature, or to cure.

11 What noble fruit the vines produce!
The olive yields a shining juice;
Our hearts are cheer'd with gen'rous wine,
With inward joy our faces shine.

12 O bless his Name ye Britons, fed
With nature's chief supporter, bread;
While bread your vital strength imparts,
Serve him with vigour in your hearts.

PAUSE II.

13 Behold the stately cedar stands,
Rais'd in the forest by his hands:
Birds to the boughs for shelter fly
And build their nests secure on high.

14 To craggy hills ascends the goat;
And at the airy mountain's foot
The feebler creatures make their cell;
He gives them wisdom where to dwell.

15 He sets the sun his circling race,
Appoints the moon to change her face;
And when thick darkness veils the day,
Calls out wild beasts to hunt their prey.

16 Fierce lions lead their young abroad,
And roaring ask their meat from God;
But when the morning beams arise,
The savage beast to covert flies.

17 Then man to daily labour goes;
The night was made for his repose:
Sleep is thy gift; that sweet relief
From tiresome toil and wasting grief.

18 How strange thy works! how great thy skill!
And every land thy riches fill:
Thy wisdom round the world we see,
This spacious earth is full of thee.

19 Nor less thy glories in the deep,
Where fish in millions swim and creep,
With wondrous motions, swift or slow,
Still wandering in the paths below.

20 There ships divide their watery way,
And flocks of scaly monsters play;
There dwells the huge Leviathan,
And foams and sports in spite of man.

PAUSE III.

21 Vast are thy works, almighty Lord,
All nature rests upon thy word,
And the whole race of creatures stands,
Waiting their portion from thy hands.

22 While each receives his different food,
Their cheerful looks pronounce it good;
Eagles and bears, and whales and worms,
Rejoice and praise in different forms.

23 But when thy face is hid, they mourn,
And dying to their dust return;
Both man and beast their souls resign,
Life, breath, and spirit, all is thine.

24 Yet thou canst breathe on dust again,
And fill the world with beasts and men;
A word of thy creating breath
Repairs the wastes of time and death.

25 His works, the wonders of his might,
Are honour'd with his own delight:
How awful are his glorious ways!
The Lord is dreadful in his praise.

26 The earth stands trembling at thy stroke,
And at thy touch the mountains smoke;
Yet humble souls may see thy face,
And tell their wants to sovereign grace.

27 In thee my hopes and wishes meet,
And make my meditations sweet:
Thy praises shall my breath employ,
Till it expire in endless joy.

28 While haughty sinners die accurst,
Their glory bury'd with their dust,
I, to my God, my heavenly King,
Immortal hallelujahs sing.

Psalm 105. Abridged.
God's conduct of Israel, and the plagues of
Egypt.

1 Give thanks to God, invoke his Name,
And tell the world his grace;
Sound thro' the earth his deeds of fame,
That all may seek his face.

2 His covenant, which he kept in mind
For numerous ages past,
To numerous ages yet behind,
In equal force shall last.

3 He sware to Abraham and his seed,
And made the blessing sure:
Gentiles the ancient promise read,
And find his truths endure.

4 "Thy seed shall make all nations blest,"
(Said the Almighty voice)
"And Canaan's land shall be their rest,
"The type of heavenly joys."

5 [How large the grant! how rich the grace!
To give them Canaan's land,
When they were strangers in the place,
A little feeble band!

6 Like pilgrims thro' the countries round
Securely they remov'd;
And haughty kings that on them frown'd,
Severely he reprov'd.

7 "Touch mine anointed, and my arm
"Shall soon revenge the wrong:
"The man that does my prophets harm
Shall know their God is strong."

8 Then let the world forbear its rage,
Nor put the church in fear:
Israel must live thro' every age,
And be th' Almighty's care.]

PAUSE I.

9 When Pharaoh dar'd to vex the saints,
And thus provok'd their God,
Moses was sent at their complaints,
Arm'd with his dreadful rod.

10 He call'd for darkness; darkness came
Like an o'erwhelming flood;
He turn'd each lake and every stream
To lakes and streams of blood.

11 He gave the sign, and noisome flies
Thro' the whole country spread;
And frogs, in croaking armies, rise
About the monarch's bed.

12 Thro' fields, and towns, and palaces,
The tenfold vengeance flew;
Locusts in swarms devour'd their trees,
And hail their cattle slew.

13 Then by an angel's midnight stroke,
The flower of Egypt dy'd;
The strength of every house was broke,
Their glory and their pride.

14 Now let the world forbear its rage,
Nor put the church in fear;
Israel must live thro' every age,
And be th' Almighty's care.

PAUSE II.

15 Thus were the tribes from bondage brought,
And left the hated ground;
Each some Egyptian spoils had got,
And not one feeble found.

16 The Lord himself chose out their way,
And mark'd their journies right,
Gave them a leading cloud by day,
A fiery guide by night.

17 They thirst; and waters from the rock
In rich abundance flow,
And following still the course they took,
Ran all the desert thro'.

18 O wondrous stream O blessed type
Of ever-flowing grace!
So Christ our rock maintains our life
Thro' all this wilderness.

19 Thus guarded by th' Almighty hand
The chosen tribes possest
Canaan the rich, the promis'd land,
And there enjoy'd their rest.

20 Then let the world forbear its rage,
The church renounce her fear;
Israel must live thro' every age,
And be th' Almighty's care.

Psalm 106:1. 1-5. First Part.
Praise to God; or, Communion with saints.

1 To God, the great, the ever blest,
Let songs of honour be addrest:
His mercy firm for ever stands;
Give him the thanks his love demands.

2 Who knows the wonders of thy ways?
Who shall fulfil thy boundless praise?
Blest are the souls that fear thee still,
And pay their duty to thy will.

3 Remember what thy mercy did
For Jacob's race, thy chosen seed;
And with the same salvation bless
The meanest suppliant of thy grace.

4 O may I see thy tribes rejoice,
And aid their triumphs with my voice!
This is my glory, Lord, to be
Join'd to thy saints, and near to thee.

Psalm 106:2. 7 8 12-14 43-48. 2d Part. Israel
punished and pardoned; or, God's unchangeable
love.

1 God of eternal love,
How fickle are our ways!
And yet how oft did Israel prove
Thy constancy of grace!

2 They saw thy wonders wrought,
And then thy praise they sung;
But soon thy works of power forgot,
And murmur'd with their tongue.

3 Now they believe his word,
While rocks with rivers flow;
Now with their lusts provoke the Lord,
And he reduc'd them low.

4 Yet when they mourn'd their faults,
He hearken'd to their groans,

Brought his own covenant to his thoughts,
And call'd them still his sons.

5 Their names were in his book,
He sav'd them from their foes;
Oft he chastis'd, but ne'er forsook
The people that he chose.

6 Let Israel bless the Lord,
Who lov'd their ancient race;
And Christians join the solemn word
Amen, to all the praise.

Psalm 107:1. First Part. Israel led to Canaan,
and Christians to Heaven.

1 Give thanks to God; he reigns above,
Kind are his thoughts, his Name is love;
His mercy ages past have known,
And ages long to come shall own.

2 Let the redeemed of the Lord
The wonders of his grace record;
Israel, the nation whom he chose,
And rescu'd from their mighty foes.

3 [When God's almighty arm had broke
Their fetters and th' Egyptian yoke,
They trac'd the desert, wandering round
A wild and solitary ground.

4 There they could find no leading road,
Nor city for a fix'd abode;
Nor food, nor fountain to assuage
Their burning thirst, or hunger's rage.]

5 In their distress to God they cry'd,
God was their Saviour and their Guide;
He led their march far wandering round,
'Twas the right path to Canaan's ground.

6 Thus when our first release we gain
From sin's old yoke, and Satan's chain,
We have this desert world to pass,
A dangerous and a tiresome place.

7 He feeds and clothes us all the way,
He guides our footsteps lest we stray,
He guards us with a powerful hand
And brings us to the heavenly land.

8 O let the saints with joy record
The truth and goodness of the Lord!
How great his works! how kind his ways!
Let every tongue pronounce his praise.

Psalm 107:2. Second Part.
Correction for sin, and release by prayer.

1 From age to age exalt his Name,
God and his grace are still the same;
He fills the hungry soul with food,
And feeds the poor with every good.

2 But if their hearts rebel and rise
Against the God that rules the skies,
If they reject his heavenly word,
And slight the counsels of the Lord,

3 He'll bring their spirits to the ground,
And no deliverer shall be found;
Laden with grief they waste their breath
In darkness and the shades of death,

4 Then to the Lord they raise their cries,
He makes the dawning light arise,
And scatters all that dismal shade,
That hung so heavy round their head.

5 He cuts the bars of brass in two,
And lets the smiling prisoners thro';
Takes off the load of guilt and grief,
And gives the labouring soul relief.

6 O may the sons of men record
The wondrous goodness of the Lord!
How great his works! how kind his ways!
Let every tongue pronounce his praise.

Psalm 107:3. Third Part.
Intemperance punished and pardoned; or,
A psalm for the glutton and the drunkard.

1 Vain man, on foolish pleasures bent,
Prepares for his own punishment;
What pains, what loathsome maladies
From luxury and lust arise!

2 The drunkard feels his vitals waste,
Yet drowns his health to please his taste;

Till all his active powers are lost,
And fainting life draws near the dust.

3 The glutton groans and loathes to eat,
His soul abhors delicious meat;
Nature, with heavy loads opprest,
Would yield to death to be releas'd.

4 Then how the frighted sinners fly
To God for help with earnest cry!
He hears their groans, prolongs their breath,
And saves them from approaching death,

5 No med'cines could effect the cure
So quick, so easy, or so sure:
The deadly sentence God repeals,
He sends his sovereign word, and heals,

6 O may the sons of men record
The wondrous goodness of the Lord!
And let their thankful offerings prove
How they adore their Maker's love.

Psalm 107:4. Fourth Part. L. M. Deliverance
from storms, and shipwreck; or, The Seaman's
song.

1 Would you behold the works of God,
His wonders in the world abroad,
Go with the mariners, and trace
The unknown regions of the seas.

2 They leave their native shores behind,
And seize the favour of the wind,
Till God command, and tempests rise
That heave the ocean to the skies.

3 Now to the heavens they mount amain,
Now sink to dreadful deeps again;
What strange affrights young sailors feel,
And like a staggering drunkard reel!

4 When land is far, and death is nigh,
Lost to all hope, to God they cry;
His mercy hears the loud address,
And sends salvation in distress.

5 He bids the winds their wrath assuage;
The furious waves forget their rage;

'Tis calm; and sailors smile to see
The haven where they wish'd to be.

6 O may the sons of men record
The wondrous goodness of the Lord!
Let them their private offerings bring,
And in the church his glory sing.

Psalm 107:5. Fourth Part. C. M.
The Mariner's psalm.

1 Thy works of glory, mighty Lord,
Thy wonders in the deeps,
The sons of courage shall record
Who trade in floating ships.

2 At thy command the winds arise,
And swell the towering waves;
The men astonish'd mount the skies
And sink in gaping graves.

3 [Again they climb the watery hills,
And plunge in deeps again;
Each like a tottering drunkard reels,
And finds his courage vain.

4 Frighted to hear the tempest roar,
They pant with fluttering breath,
And, hopeless of the distant shore,
Expect immediate death.]

5 Then to the Lord they raise their cries,
He hears the loud request,
And orders silence thro' the skies,
And lays the floods to rest.

6 Sailors rejoice to lose their fears,
And see the storm allay'd:
Now to their eyes the port appears;
There let their vows be paid.

7 'Tis God that brings them safe to land;
Let stupid mortals know
That waves are under his command,
And all the winds that blow,

8 O that the sons of men would praise
The goodness of the Lord!
And those that see thy wondrous ways,
Thy wondrous love record.

Psalm 107:6. Last Part.
Colonies planted; or,
Nations blest and punished.

A psalm for New England.

1 When God, provok'd with daring crimes,
Scourges the madness of the times,
He turns their fields to barren sand,
And dries the rivers from the land.

2 His word can raise the springs again,
And make the wither'd mountains green,
Send showery blessings from the skies,
And harvests in the desert rise.

3 [Where nothing dwelt but beasts of prey,
Or men as fierce and wild as they;
He bids th' opprest and poor repair,
And builds them towns and cities there.

4 They sow the fields, and trees they plant,
Whose yearly fruit supplies their want:
Their race grows up from fruitful stocks,
Their wealth increases with their flocks.

5 Thus they are blest; but if they sin,
He lets the heathen nations in,
A savage crew invades their lands,
Their princes die by barbarous hands.

6 Their captive sons, expos'd to scorn,
Wander unpity'd and forlorn;
The country lies unfenc'd, untill'd,
And desolation spreads the field.

7 Yet if the humbled nation mourns,
Again his dreadful hand he turns;
Again he makes their cities thrive,
And bids the dying churches live.]

8 The righteous, with a joyful sense,
Admire the works of providence;
And tongues of atheists shall no more
Blaspheme the God that saints adore.

9 How few, with pious care, record
The wondrous dealings of the Lord!
But wise observers still shall find
The Lord is holy, just, and kind.

Psalm 109. 1-5 31.
Love to enemies, from the example of Christ.

1 God of my mercy and my praise,
Thy glory is my song;
The sinners speak against thy grace
With a blaspheming tongue.

2 When in the form of mortal man
Thy Son on earth was found,
With cruel slanders, false and vain,
They compass'd him around.

3 Their miseries his compassion move,
Their peace he still pursu'd;
They render hatred for his love,
And evil for his good.

4 Their malice rag'd without a cause,
Yet, with his dying breath,
He pray'd for murderers on his cross,
And blest his foes in death.

5 Lord, shall thy bright example shine
In vain before my eyes?
Give me a soul a-kin to thine
To love mine enemies.

6 The Lord shall on my side engage,
And, in my Saviour's name,
I shall defeat their pride and rage
Who slander and condemn.

Psalm 110:1. First Part. Christ exalted, and
multitudes converted; or, The success of the
gospel.

1 Thus the eternal Father spake
To Christ the Son, "Ascend and sit
"At my right hand, till I shall make
"Thy foes submissive at thy feet.

2 "From Zion shall thy word proceed,
"Thy word, the sceptre in thy hand,
"Shall make the hearts of rebels bleed,
"And bow their wills to thy command.

3 "That day shall shew thy power is great,
"When saints shall flock with willing minds,

"And sinners crowd thy temple gate,
"Where holiness in beauty shines."

4 O blessed power! 0 glorious day!
What a large victory shall ensue!
And converts, who thy grace obey,
Exceed the drops of morning dew.

Psalm 110:2. Second Part.
The kingdom and priesthood of Christ.

1 Thus the great Lord of earth and sea
Spake to his Son, and thus he swore;
"Eternal shall thy priesthood be,
"And change from hand to hand no more.

2 "Aaron and all his sons must die;
"But everlasting life is thine,
"To save for ever those that fly
"For refuge from the wrath divine.

3 "By me Melchisedek was made
"On earth a king and priest at once;
"And thou, my heavenly priest, shalt plead,
"And thou, my king, shalt rule my sons."

4 Jesus the priest ascends his throne,
While counsels of eternal peace,
Between the Father and the Son,
Proceed with honour and success.

5 Thro' the whole earth his reign shall spread,
And crush the powers that dare rebel;
Then shall he judge the rising dead,
And send the guilty world to hell.

6 Tho' while he treads his glorious way,
He drink the cup of tears and blood,
The sufferings of that dreadful day
Shall but advance him near to God.

Psalm 110:3. C. M.
Christ's kingdom and priesthood.

1 Jesus, our Lord, ascend thy throne,
And near the Father sit;
In Zion shall thy power be known,
And make thy foes submit.

2 What wonders shall thy gospel do!
Thy converts shall surpass
The numerous drops of morning dew,
And own thy sovereign grace.

3 God hath pronounc'd a firm decree,
Nor changes what he swore;
"Eternal shall thy priesthood be,
"When Aaron is no more.

4 "Melchisedek, that wondrous priest,
"That king of high degree,
"That holy man who Abr'am blest,
"Was but a type of thee."

5 Jesus our priest for ever lives
To plead for us above;
Jesus our king for ever gives
The blessings of his love.

6 God shall exalt his glorious head,
And his high throne maintain,
Shall strike the powers and princes dead
Who dare oppose his reign.

Psalm 111:1. First Part.
The wisdom of God in his works.

1 Songs of immortal praise belong
To my almighty God;
He has my heart, and he my tongue
To spread his Name abroad.

2 How great the works his hand has wrought!
How glorious in our sight!
And men in every age have sought
His wonders with delight.

3 How most exact is nature's frame!
How wise th' Eternal mind!
His counsels never change the scheme
That his first thoughts design'd.

4 When he redeem'd his chosen Son,
He fix'd his covenant sure:
The orders that his lips pronounce
To endless years endure.

5 Nature and time, and earth and skies,
Thy heavenly skill proclaim:

What shall we do to make us wise,
But learn to read thy Name?

6 To fear thy power, to trust thy grace
Is our divinest skill;
And he's the wisest of our race,
That best obeys thy will.

Psalm 111:2. Second Part.
The perfections of God.

1 Great is the Lord; his works of might
Demand our noblest songs;
Let his assembled saints unite
Their harmony of tongues.

2 Great is the mercy of the Lord,
He gives his children food;
And ever mindful of his word,
He makes his promise good.

3 His Son, the great Redeemer, came
To seal his covenant sure:
Holy and reverend is his Name,
His ways are just and pure.

4 They that would grow divinely wise
Must with his fear begin;
Our fairest proof of knowledge lies
In hating every sin.

Psalm 112:1. As the 113th Psalm.
The blessings of the liberal man.

1 That man is blest who stands in awe
Of God, and loves his sacred law:
His seed on earth shall be renown'd;
His house the seat of wealth shall be,
An inexhausted treasury,
And with successive honours crown'd.

2 His liberal favours he extends,
To some he gives, to others lends;
A generous pity fills his mind:
Yet what his charity impairs
He saves by prudence in affairs,
And thus he's just to all mankind.

3 His hands, while they his alms bestow'd,
His glory's future harvest sow'd;
The sweet remembrance of the just,
Like a green root, revives and bears
A train of blessings for his heirs,
When dying nature sleeps in dust.

4 Beset with threatening dangers round,
Unmov'd shall he maintain his ground;
His conscience holds his courage up:
The soul that's fill'd with virtue's light,
Shines brightest in affliction's night,
And sees in darkness beams of hope.

PAUSE.

5 [Ill tidings never can surprise
His heart that fix'd on God relies,
Tho' waves and tempests roar around:
Safe on the rock he sits, and sees
The shipwreck of his enemies,
And all their hope and glory drown'd.

6 The wicked shall his triumph see,
And gnash their teeth in agony
To find their expectations crost:
They and their envy, pride and spite,
Sink down to everlasting night,
And all their names in darkness lost.]

Psalm 112:2. L. M.
The blessings of the pious and charitable.

1 Thrice happy man who fears the Lord,
Loves his commands, and trusts his word;
Honour and peace his days attend,
And blessings to his seed descend.

2 Compassion dwells upon his mind,
To works of mercy still inclin'd:
He lends the poor some present aid,
Or gives them, not to be repaid.

3 When times grow dark, and tidings spread
That fill his neighbours round with dread,
His heart is arm'd against the fear,
For God with all his power is there.

4 His soul, well fix'd upon the Lord,
Draws heavenly courage from his word;

Amidst the darkness light shall rise,
To cheer his heart, and bless his eyes.

5 He hath dispers'd his alms abroad,
His works are still before his God;
His name on earth shall long remain,
While envious sinners fret in vain.

Psalm 112:3. C. M,
Liberality rewarded.

1 Happy is he that fears the Lord,
And follows his commands,
Who lends the poor without reward,
Or gives with liberal hands.

2 As pity dwells within his breast
To all the sons of need;
So God shall answer his request
With blessings on his seed,

3 No evil tidings shall surprise
His well-establish'd mind;
His soul to God his refuge flies,
And leaves his fears behind.

4 In times of general distress,
Some beams of light shall shine
To shew the world his righteousness,
And give him peace divine.

5 His works of piety and love
Remain before the Lord;
Honour on earth and joys above
Shall be his sure reward.

Psalm 113:1. Proper Time.
The majesty and condescension of God.

1 Ye that delight to serve the Lord,
The honours of his Name record,
His sacred Name for ever bless:
Where'er the circling sun displays
His rising beams, or setting rays,
Let lands and seas his power confess.

2 Not time, nor nature's narrow rounds,
Can give his vast dominion bounds,
The heavens are far below his height:

Let no created greatness dare
With our eternal God compare,
Arm'd with his uncreated might.

3 He bows his glorious head to view
What the bright hosts of angels do,
And bends his care to mortal things;
His sovereign hand exalts the poor,
He takes the needy from the door,
And makes them company for kings.

4 When childless families despair,
He sends the blessings of an heir
To rescue their expiring name:
The mother with a thankful voice
Proclaims his praises and her joys:
Let every age advance his fame.

Psalm 113:2. L. M.
God sovereign and gracious.

1 Ye servants of th' Almighty King,
In every age his praises sing;
Where'er the sun shall rise or set,
The nations shall his praise repeat.

2 Above the earth, beyond the sky,
Stands his high throne of majesty:
Nor time, nor place, his power restrain,
Nor bound his universal reign.

3 Which of the sons of Adam dare,
Or angels, with their God compare?
His glories how divinely bright,
Who dwells in uncreated light!

4 Behold his love: he stoops to view
What saints above and angels do;
And condescends yet more to know
The mean affairs of men below.

5 From dust and cottages obscure
His grace exalts the humble poor;
Gives them the honour of his sons,
And fits them for their heavenly thrones.

6 [A word of his creating voice
Can make the barren house rejoice:
Tho' Sarah's ninety years were past,
The promis'd seed is born at last.

7 With joy the mother views her son,
And tells the wonders God has done:
Faith may grow strong when sense despairs,
If nature fails, the promise bears.]

Psalm 114.
Miracles attending Israel's journey.

1 When Israel, freed from Pharaoh's hand,
Left the proud tyrant and his land,
The tribes with cheerful homage own
Their King, and Judah was his throne.

2 Across the deep their journey lay;
The deep divides to make them way:
Jordan beheld their march, and fled
With backward current to his head.

3 The mountains shook like frighted sheep,
Like lambs the little hillocks leap;
Not Sinai on her base could stand,
Conscious of sovereign power at hand.

4 What power could make the deep divide?
Make Jordan backward roll his tide?
Why did ye leap, ye little hills?
And whence the fright that Sinai feels?

5 Let every mountain, every flood,
Retire and know th' approaching God,
The king of Israel: see him here;
Tremble, thou earth, adore and fear.

6 He thunders, and all nature mourns,
The rock to standing pools he turns;
Flints spring with fountains at his word,
And fires and seas confess the Lord.

Psalm 115:1. First Metre. The true God our
refuge; or, Idolatry reproved.

1 Not to ourselves, who are but dust,
Not to ourselves is glory due,
Eternal God, thou only just,
Thou only gracious, wise, and true.

2 Shine forth in all thy dreadful Name;
Why should a heathen's haughty tongue

Insult us, and to raise our shame
Say, "Where's the God you've serv'd so long?"

3 The God we serve maintains his throne
Above the clouds, beyond the skies,
Thro' all the earth his will is done,
He knows our groans, he hears our cries.

4 But the vain idols they adore
Are senseless shapes of stone and wood;
At best a mass of glittering ore,
A silver saint, or golden god.

5 [With eyes, and ears they carve their head,
Deaf are their ears, their eyes are blind;
In vain are costly offerings made,
And vows are scatter'd in the wind.

6 Their feet were never made to move,
Nor hands to save when mortals pray;
Mortals that pay them fear or love
Seem to be blind and deaf as they.]

7 O Israel, make the Lord thy hope,
Thy help, thy refuge, and thy rest;
The Lord shall build thy ruins up,
And bless the people and the priest.

8 The dead no more can speak thy praise,
They dwell in silence and the grave;
But we shall live to sing thy grace,
And tell the world thy power to save.

Psalm 115:2. Second Metre.
As the new tune of the 50th Psalm.
Popish idolatry reproved.

A psalm for the 5th of November.

1 Not to our names, thou only Just and True,
Not to our worthless names is glory due;
Thy power and grace, thy truth and justice claim
Immortal honours to thy sovereign Name:
Shine thro' the earth from heaven, thy blest
abode,
Nor let the heathens say, "And where's your
God?"

2 Heaven is thine higher court; there stands thy
throne,

And thro' the lower worlds thy will is done:
Our God fram'd all this earth, these heavens he
spread,
But fools adore the gods their hands have made:
The kneeling crowd, with looks devout, behold
Their silver saviours, and their saints of gold.

3 [Vain are those artful shapes of eyes and ears;
The molten image neither sees nor hears:
Their hands are helpless, nor their feet can
move,
They have no speech, nor thought, nor power,
nor love;
Yet sottish mortals make their long complaints
To their deaf idols, and their moveless saints.

4 The rich have statues well adorn'd with gold;
The poor, content with gods of coarser mould,
With tools of iron carve the senseless stock,
Lopt from a tree, or broken from a rock:
People and priest drive on the solemn trade,
And trust the gods that saws and hammers
made.]

5 Be heaven and earth amaz'd! 'Tis hard to say
Which is more stupid, or their gods or they:
O Israel, trust the Lord, he hears and sees,
He knows thy sorrows, and restores thy peace:
His worship does a thousand comforts yield,
He is thy help, and he thy heavenly shield.

6 O Britain, trust the Lord: thy foes in vain
Attempt thy ruin, and oppose his reign;
Had they prevail'd, darkness had clos'd our
days,
And death and silence had forbid his praise;
But we are sav'd, and live: let songs arise,
And Britain bless the God that built the skies.

Psalm 116:1. First Part.
Recovery from sickness.

1 I love the Lord; he heard my cries,
And pity'd every groan:
Long as I live, when troubles rise,
I'll hasten to his throne.

2 I love the Lord; he bow'd his ear,
And chas'd my griefs away;

O let my heart no more despair,
While I have breath to pray!

3 My flesh declin'd, my spirits fell,
And I drew near the dead,
While inward pangs, and fears of hell
Perplex'd my wakeful head.

4 "My God," I cry'd "thy servant save,
"Thou ever good and just;
"Thy power can rescue from the grave,
"Thy power is all my trust."

5 The Lord beheld me sore distrest,
He bid my pains remove:
Return, my soul, to God thy rest,
For thou hast known his love.

6 My God hath sav'd my soul from death,
And dry'd my failing tears;
Now to his praise I'll spend my breath,
And my remaining years.

Psalm 116:2. 12 &c. Second Part. Vows made
in trouble paid in the church; or, Public thanks
for private deliverance.

1 What shall I render to my God
For all his kindness shown?
My feet shall visit thine abode,
My songs address thy throne.

2 Among the saints that fill thine house,
My offerings shall be paid;
There shall my zeal perform the vows
My soul in anguish made.

3 How much is mercy thy delight,
Thou ever blessed God!
How dear thy servants in thy sight!
How precious is their blood!

4 How happy all thy servants are!
How great thy grace to me!
My life which thou hast made thy care,
Lord, I devote to thee.

5 Now I am thine, for ever thine,
Nor shall my purpose move;

Thy hand hath loos'd my bonds of pain,
And bound me with thy love.

6 Here in thy courts I leave my vow,
And thy rich grace record;
Witness, ye saints, who hear me now,
If I forsake the Lord.

Psalm 117:1. C. M.
Praise to God from all nations.

1 O all ye nations, praise the Lord,
Each with a different tongue;
In every language learn his word,
And let his Name be sung.

2 His mercy reigns thro' every land;
Proclaim his grace abroad;
For ever firm his truth shall stand,
Praise ye the faithful God.

Psalm 117:2. L. M.

1 From all that dwell below the skies,
Let the Creator's praise arise!
Let the Redeemer's name be sung
Thro' every land, by every tongue.

2 Eternal are thy mercies, Lord;
Eternal truth attends thy word:
Thy praise shall sound from shore to shore,
Till suns shall rise and set no more.

Psalm 117:3. S. M.

1 Thy Name, almighty Lord,
Shall sound thro' distant lands;
Great is thy grace, and sure thy word,
Thy truth for ever stands.

2 Far be thine honour spread,
And long thy praise endure,
Till morning light and evening shade
Shall be exchang'd no more.

Psalm 118:1. 6-15. First Part.
Deliverance from a tumult.

1 The Lord appears my helper now,
Nor is my faith afraid
What all the sons of earth can do,
Since heaven affords its aid.

2 'Tis safer, Lord, to hope in thee,
And have my God my friend,
Than trust in men of high degree,
And on their truth depend.

3 Like bees my foes beset me round,
A large and angry swarm;
But I shall all their rage confound
By thine almighty arm.

4 'Tis thro' the Lord my heart is strong,
In him my lips rejoice;
While his salvation is my song,
How cheerful is my voice!

5 Like angry bees they girt me round;
When God appears they fly:
So burning thorns, with crackling sound,
Make a fierce blaze and die.

6 Joy to the saints and peace belongs;
The Lord protects their days:
Let Israel tune immortal songs
To his almighty grace.

Psalm 118:2. 17-21. Second Part.
Public praise for deliverance from death.

1 Lord, thou hast heard thy servant cry,
And rescu'd from the grave;
Now shall he live: (and none can die
If God resolve to save.)

2 Thy praise, more constant than before,
Shall fill his daily breath;
Thy hand that hath chastis'd him sore,
Defends him still from death.

3 Open the gates of Zion now,
For we shall worship there,
The house where all the righteous go
Thy mercy to declare.

4 Among th' assemblies of thy saints
Our thankful voice we raise!

There we have told thee our complaints,
And there we speak thy praise.

Psalm 118:3. 22 23. Third Part.
Christ the foundation of his church.

1 Behold the sure foundation-stone
Which God in Zion lays
To build our heavenly hopes upon,
And his eternal praise.

2 Chosen of God, to sinners dear,
And saints adore the Name,
They trust their whole salvation here,
Nor shall they suffer shame.

3 The foolish builders, scribe and priest,
Reject it with disdain;
Yet on this rock the church shall rest,
And envy rage in vain.

4 What tho' the gates of hell withstood,
Yet must this building rise:
'Tis thy own work, almighty God,
And wondrous in our eyes.

Psalm 118:4. 24 25 26. Fourth Part. Hosanna;
the Lord's day; or, Christ's resurrection and our
salvation.

1 This is the day the Lord hath made,
He calls the hours his own;
Let heaven rejoice, let earth be glad,
And praise surround the throne.

2 To-day he rose and left the dead,
And Satan's empire fell;
To-day the saints his triumphs spread,
And all his wonders tell.

3 Hosanna to th' anointed King,
To David's holy Son:
Help us, O Lord; descend and bring
Salvation from the throne.

4 Blest be the Lord, who comes to men
With messages of grace;
Who comes in God his Father's Name
To save our sinful race.

5 Hosanna in the highest strains
The church on earth can raise;
The highest heavens, in which he reigns,
Shall give him nobler praise.

Psalm 118:5. 22-27. S. M.
An hosanna for the Lord's day; or,
A new song of salvation by Christ.

1 See what a living-stone
The builders did refuse:
Yet God hath built his church thereon
In spite of envious Jews.

2 The scribe and angry priest
Reject thine only Son;
Yet on this rock shall Zion rest,
As the chief corner-stone.

3 The work, O Lord, is thine,
And wondrous in our eyes;
This day declares it all divine,
This day did Jesus rise.

4 This is the glorious day
That our Redeemer made;
Let us rejoice, and sing, and pray,
Let all the church be glad.

5 Hosanna to the King
Of David's royal blood:
Bless him, ye saints; he comes to bring
Salvation from your God.

6 We bless thine holy word,
Which all this grace displays;
And offer on thine altar, Lord,
Our sacrifice of praise.

Psalm 118:6. 22-27. L. M.
An hosanna for the Lord's day; or,
A new song of salvation by Christ.

1 Lo! what a glorious corner-stone
The Jewish builders did refuse;
But God hath built his church thereon,
In spite of envy and the Jews.

2 Great God, the work is all divine,
The joy and wonder of our eyes;
This is the day that proves it thine,
The day that saw our Saviour rise.

3 Sinners rejoice, and saints be glad:
Hosanna, let his Name be blest:
A thousand honours on his head,
With peace, and light, and glory, rest.

4 In God's own name he comes to bring
Salvation to our dying race:
Let the whole church address their King
With hearts of joy, and songs of praise.

Psalm 119. I have collected and disposed the
most useful verses of this psalm under eighteen
different heads, and formed a divine song upon
each of them. But the verses are much
transposed to attain some degree of connection.

In some places, among the words "law,"
"commands," "judgments," "testimonies," I
have used "gospel," "word," "grace," "truth,"
"promises," &c. as more agreeable to the
language of the New Testament, and the
common language of Christians, and it equally
answers the design of the Psalmist, which was
to recommend the holy scripture.

Psalm 119:01. First Part.
The blessedness of saints, and misery of sinners.

Ver. 1 2 3.
1 Blest are the undefil'd in heart,
Whose ways are right and clean;
Who never from thy law depart,
But fly front every sin.

2 Blest are the men that keep thy word,
And practise thy commands;
With their whole heart they seek the Lord,
And serve thee with their hands.

Ver. 165.
3 Great is their peace who love thy law;
How firm their souls abide!
Nor can a bold temptation draw
Their steady feet aside.

Ver. 6.
4 Then shall my heart have inward joy,
And keep my face from shame,
When all thy statutes I obey,
And honour all thy name.

Ver. 21 118.
5 But haughty sinners God will hate,
The proud shall die accurst;
The sons of falsehood and deceit
Are trodden to the dust.

Ver. 119 155.
6 Vile as the dross the wicked are;
And those that leave thy ways
Shall see salvation from afar,
But never taste thy grace.

Psalm 119:02. Second Part. Secret devotion and
spiritual mindedness; or, Constant converse
with God.

Ver. 147 55.
1 TO thee, before the dawning light,
My gracious God, I pray;
I meditate thy Name by night,
And keep thy law by day.

Ver. 81.
2 My spirit faints to see thy grace,
Thy promise bears me up;
And while salvation long delays,
Thy word supports my hope.

Ver. 164.
3 Seven times a day I lift my hands,
And pay my thanks to thee;
Thy righteous providence demands
Repeated praise from me.

Ver. 62.
4 When midnight darkness veils the skies,
I call thy works to mind;
My thoughts in warm devotion rise,
And sweet acceptance find.

Psalm 119:03. Third Part.
Profession: of sincerity, repentance, and
obedience.

Ver. 57 60.
1 Thou art my portion, O my God;
Soon as I know thy way,
My heart makes haste t' obey thy word,
And suffers no delay.

Ver. 30 14.
2 I choose the path of heavenly truth,
And glory in my choice:
Not all the riches of the earth
Could make me so rejoice.

3 The testimonies of thy grace
I set before my eyes;
Thence I derive my daily strength,
And there my comfort lies.

Ver. 59.
4 If once I wander from thy path,
I think upon my ways,
Then turn my feet to thy commands,
And trust thy pardoning grace.

Ver. 94 114.
5 Now I am thine, for ever thine,
O save thy servant, Lord;
Thou art my shield, my hiding-place,
My hope is in thy word.

Ver. 112.
6 Thou hast inclin'd this heart of mine,
Thy statutes to fulfil;
And thus till mortal life shall end
Would I perform thy will.

Ver. 105.
3 'Tis like the sun, a heavenly light,
That guides us all the day;
And thro' the dangers of the night,
A lamp to lead our way.

Ver. 99 100.
4 The men that keep thy law with care,
And meditate thy word,
Grow wiser than their teachers are,
And better know the Lord.

Ver. 104 113.
5 Thy precepts make me truly wise:
I hate the sinner's road;
I hate my own vain thoughts that rise,
But love thy law, my God.

Ver. 89 90 91.
6 [The starry heavens thy rule obey,
The earth maintains her place;
And these thy servants night and day
Thy skill and power express!

7 But still thy law and gospel, Lord,
Have lessons more divine;
Not earth stands firmer than thy word,
Nor stars so nobly shine.]

Ver. 160 140 9 116.
8 Thy word is everlasting truth;
How pure is every page!
That holy book shall guide our youth,
And well support our age.

Psalm 119:04. Fourth Part.
Instruction from scripture.

Ver. 9.
1 How shall the young secure their hearts,
And guard their lives from sin?
Thy word the choicest rules imparts
To keep the conscience clean.

Ver. 130.
2 When once it enters to the mind,
It spreads such light abroad,
The meanest souls instruction find,
And raise their thoughts to God.

Psalm 119:05. Fifth Part. Delight in scripture;
or, The word of God dwelling in us.

Ver. 97.
1 O How I love thy holy law!
'Tis daily my delight;
And thence my meditations draw
Divine advice by night.

Ver. 148.
2 My waking eyes prevent the day
To meditate thy word;
My soul with longing melts away
To hear thy gospel, Lord.

Ver. 3 13 54.
3 How doth thy word my heart engage!
How well employ my tongue!
And, in my tiresome pilgrimage,
Yields me a heavenly song.

Ver. 19 103.
4 Am I a stranger, or at home,
'Tis my perpetual feast;
Not honey dropping from the comb
So much allures the taste.

Ver. 72 127.
5 No treasures so enrich the mind;
Nor shall thy word be sold
For loads of silver well refin'd,
Nor heaps of choicest gold.

Ver. 28 49 175.
6 When nature sinks, and spirits droop,
Thy promises of grace
Are pillars to support my hope,
And there I write thy praise.

Psalm 119:06. Sixth Part.
Holiness and comfort from the word.

Ver. 128.
1 Lord, I esteem thy judgments right,
And all thy statutes just;
Thence I maintain a constant fight
With every flattering lust.

Ver. 97 9.
2 Thy precepts often I survey;
I keep thy law in sight,
Thro' all the business of the day,
To form my actions right.

Ver. 62.
3 My heart in midnight silence cries,
"How sweet thy comforts be!"
My thoughts in holy wonder rise,
And bring their thanks to thee.

Ver. 162.
4 And when my spirit drinks her fill
At some good word of thine,
Not mighty men that share the spoil
Have joys compar'd to mine.

Psalm 119:07. Seventh Part. Imperfection of
nature, and perfection of scripture.

Ver. 96. paraphrased.
1 Let all the heathen writers join
To form one perfect book,
Great God, if once compar'd with thine,
How mean their writings look!

2 Not the most perfect rules they gave
Could shew one sin forgiven,
Nor lead a step beyond the grave;
But thine conduct to heaven.

3 I've seen an end of what we call
Perfection here below;
How short the powers of nature fall,
And can no farther go!

4 Yet men would fain be just with God
By works their hands have wrought;
But thy commands, exceeding broad,
Extend to every thought.

5 In vain we boast perfection here,
While sin defiles our frame,
And sinks our virtues down so far,
They scarce deserve the name.

6 Our faith and love, and every grace,
Fall far below thy word;
But perfect truth and righteousness
Dwell only with the Lord.

Psalm 119:08. Eighth Part.
The word of God is the saint's portion; or,
The excellency and variety of scripture.

Ver. 111. paraphrased.
1 Lord, I have made thy word my choice,
My lasting heritage;
There shall my noblest powers rejoice,
My warmest thoughts engage.

2 I'll read the histories of thy love,
And keep thy laws in sight,
While thro' the promises I rove,
With ever fresh delight.

3 'Tis a broad land of wealth unknown
Where springs of life arise,
Seeds of immortal bliss are sown,
And hidden glory lies.

4 The best relief that mourners have,
It makes our sorrows blest;
Our fairest hope beyond the grave,
And our eternal rest.

Psalm 119:09. Ninth Part. Desire of knowledge;
or, The teachings of the Spirit with the word.

Ver. 64 66 18.
1 Thy mercies fill the earth, O Lord,
How good thy works appear!
Open mine eyes to read thy word,
And see thy wonders there.

Ver. 73 125.
2 My heart was fashion'd by thy hand,
My service is thy due:
O make thy servant understand
The duties he must do.

Ver. 19.
3 Since I'm a stranger here below,
Let not thy path be hid;
But mark the road my feet should go,
And be my constant guide.

Ver. 26.
4 When I confess'd my wandering ways,
Thou heardst my soul complain;
Grant me the teachings of thy grace,
Or I shall stray again.

Ver. 33 34.
5 If God to me his statutes shew,
And heavenly truth impart,
His work for ever I'll pursue,
His laws shall rule my heart.

Ver. 50 71.
6 This was my comfort when I bore
Variety of grief;
It made me learn thy word the more,
And fly to that relief.

Ver. 51.
7 [In vain the proud deride me now;
I'll ne'er forget thy law,
Nor let that blessed gospel go
Whence all my hopes I draw.

Ver. 27 121.
8 When I have learn'd my Father's will
I'll teach the world his ways;
My thankful lips inspir'd with zeal
Shall loud pronounce his praise.]

Psalm 119:10. Tenth Part.
Pleading the promises.

Ver. 38 49.
1 Behold thy waiting servant, Lord,
Devoted to thy fear;
Remember and confirm thy word,
For all my hopes are there.

Ver. 41 58 107.
2 Hast thou not writ salvation down,
And promis'd quickening grace?
Doth not my heart address thy throne?
And yet thy love delays.

Ver. 132 42.
3 Mine eyes for thy salvation fail;
O bear thy servant up;
Nor let the scoffing lips prevail,
Who dare reproach my hope.

Ver. 49 74.
4 Didst thou not raise my faith, O Lord?
Then let thy truth appear:
Saints shall rejoice in my reward,
And trust as well as fear.

Psalm 119:11. Eleventh Part.
Breathing after holiness.

Ver. 5 33.
1 O that the Lord would guide my ways
To keep his statutes still!
O that my God would grant me grace
To know and do his will!

Ver. 29.
2 O send thy Spirit down to write
Thy law upon my heart!
Nor let my tongue indulge deceit,
Nor act the liar's part.

Ver. 37 36.
3 From vanity turn off my eyes:
Let no corrupt design,
Nor covetous desires arise
Within this soul of mine.

Ver. 133.
4 Order my footsteps by thy word,
And make my heart sincere,
Let sin have no dominion, Lord,
But keep my conscience clear.

Ver. 176.
5 My soul hath gone too far astray,
My feet too often slip;
Yet since I've not forgot thy way,
Restore thy wandering sheep.

Ver. 35.
6 Make me to walk in thy commands,
'Tis a delightful road;
Nor let my head, or heart, or hands,
Offend against my God.

Psalm 119:12. Twelfth Part.
Breathing after comfort and deliverance.

Ver. 153.
1 My God, consider my distress,
Let mercy plead my cause;
Tho' I have sinn'd against thy grace,
I can't forget thy laws.

Ver. 39 116.
1 Forbid, forbid the sharp reproach
Which I so justly fear;
Uphold my life, uphold my hopes,
Nor let my shame appear.

Ver. 122 135.
3 Be thou a surety, Lord, for me,
Nor let the proud oppress;
But make thy waiting servant see
The shinings of thy face.

Ver. 82.
4 My eyes with expectation fail,
My heart within me cries,
"When will the Lord his truth fulfil,
"And make my comforts rise?"

Ver. 132.
5 Look down upon my sorrows, Lord,
And shew thy grace the same
As thou art ever wont t' afford
To those that love thy Name.

Psalm 119:13. Thirteenth Part.
Holy fear, and tenderness of conscience.

Ver. 10.
1 With my whole heart I've sought thy face,
O let me never stray
From thy commands, O God of grace,
Nor tread the sinner's way.

Ver. 11.
2 Thy word I've hid within my heart
To keep my conscience clean,
And be an everlasting guard
From every rising sin.

Ver. 63 53 158.
3 I'm a companion of the saints
Who fear and love the Lord;
My sorrows rise, my nature faints,
When men transgress thy word.

Ver. 161 163.
4 While sinners do thy gospel wrong,
My spirit stands in awe;
My soul abhors a lying tongue,
But loves thy righteous law.

Ver. 161 120.
5 My heart with sacred reverence hears
The threatenings of thy word:
My flesh with holy trembling fears
The judgments of the Lord.

Ver. 166 174.
6 My God, I long, I hope, I wait
For thy salvation still;
While thy whole law is my delight,
And I obey thy will.

Psalm 119:14. Fourteenth Part.
Benefit of afflictions, and support under them.

Ver. 153 81 82.
1 Consider all my sorrows, Lord,
And thy deliverance send;
My soul for thy salvation faints,
When will my troubles end?

Ver. 71.
2 Yet I have found, 'tis good for me
To bear my Father's rod;
Afflictions make me learn thy law,
And live upon my God.

Ver. 50.
3 This is the comfort I enjoy
When new distress begins,
I read thy word, I run thy way,
And hate my former sins.

Ver. 92.
4 Had not thy word been my delight
When earthly joys were fled,
My soul opprest with sorrow's weight
Had sunk amongst the dead.

Ver. 75.
5 I know thy judgments, Lord, are right,
Tho' they may seem severe;
The sharpest sufferings I endure
Flow from thy faithful care.

Ver. 67.
6 Before I knew thy chastening rod
My feet were apt to stray;
But now I learn to keep thy word,
Nor wander from thy way.

Psalm 119:15. Fifteenth Part.
Holy resolutions.

Ver. 93.
That thy statutes every hour
Might dwell upon my mind!
Thence I derive a quickening power,
And daily peace I find.

Ver. 15 16.
2 To meditate thy precepts, Lord,

Shall be my sweet employ;
My soul shall ne'er forget thy word,
Thy word is all my joy.

Ver. 32.
3 How would I run in thy commands,
If thou my heart discharge
From sin and Satan's hateful chains,
And set my feet at large!

Ver. 13 46.
4 My lips with courage shall declare
Thy statutes and thy Name;
I'll speak thy word, tho' kings should hear
Nor yield to sinful shame.

Ver. 61 69 70.
5 Let bands of persecutors rise
To rob me of my right,
Let pride and malice forge their lies,
Thy law is my delight.

Ver. 115.
6 Depart from me, ye wicked race,
Whose hands and hearts are ill;
I love my God, I love his ways,
And must obey his will.

Psalm 119:16. Sixteenth Part.
Prayer for quickening grace.

Ver. 25 37.
1 My soul lies cleaving to the dust;
Lord, give me life divine;
From vain desires and every lust
Turn off these eyes of mine.

2 I need the influence of thy grace
To speed me in thy way,
Lest I should loiter in my race,
Or turn my feet astray.

Ver. 107. 3 When sore afflictions press me
down, I need thy quickening powers; Thy word
that I have rested on shall help my heaviest
hours.

Ver. 156 140.
4 Are not thy mercies sovereign still?
And thou a faithful God?

Wilt thou not grant me warmer zeal
To run the heavenly road?

Ver. 159 40.
5 Does not my heart thy precepts love,
And long to see thy face?
And yet how slow my spirits move
Without enlivening grace!

Ver. 93.
6 Then shall I love thy gospel more,
And ne'er forget thy word,
When I have felt its quickening power
To draw me near the Lord.

Psalm 119:17. Seventeenth Part. Courage and
perseverance under persecution; or, Grace
shining in difficulties and trials.

Ver. 143 28.
1 When pain and anguish seize me, Lord,
All my support is from thy word:
My soul dissolves for heaviness,
Uphold me with thy strengthening grace.

Ver. 51 69 110.
2 The proud have fram'd their scoffs and lies,
They watch my feet with envious eyes,
And tempt my soul to snares and sin,
Yet thy commands I ne'er decline.

Ver. 161 78.
3 They hate me, Lord, without a cause,
They hate to see me love thy laws:
But I will trust and fear thy Name,
Till pride and malice die with shame.

Psalm 119:18. Last Part.
Sanctified afflictions; or,
Delight in the word of God.

Ver. 67 59.
1 Father, I bless thy gentle hand;
How kind was thy chastising rod,
That forc'd my conscience to a stand,
And brought my wandering soul to God!

2 Foolish and vain I went astray
Ere I had felt thy scourges, Lord,

I left my guide, and lost my way;
But now I love and keep thy word.

Ver. 71.
3 'Tis good for me to wear the yoke,
For pride is apt to rise and swell;
'Tis good to bear my Father's stroke,
That I might learn his statutes well.

Ver. 72.
4 The law that issues from thy mouth
Shall raise my cheerful passions more
Than all the treasures of the south,
Or western hills of golden ore.

Ver. 73.
5 Thy hands have made my mortal frame,
Thy spirit form'd my soul within;
Teach me to know thy wondrous Name,
And guard me safe from death and sin.

Ver. 74.
6 Then all that love and fear the Lord
At my salvation shall rejoice;
For I have hoped in thy word,
And made thy grace my only choice.

Psalm 120. Complaint of quarrelsome
neighbours; or, A devout wish for peace.

1 Thou God of love, thou ever blest,
Pity my suffering state;
When wilt thou set my soul at rest
From lips that love deceit?

2 Hard lot of mine! my days are cast
Among the sons of strife,
Whose never-ceasing brawlings waste
My golden hours of life.

3 O might I fly to change my place,
How would I chuse to dwell
In some wide lonesome wilderness,
And leave these gates of hell.

4 Peace is the blessing that I seek,
How lovely are its charms;
I am for peace; but when I speak,
They all declare for arms.

6 New passions still their souls engage,
And keep their malice strong:
What shall be done to curb thy rage,
O thou devouring tongue!

6 Should burning arrows smite thee thro',
Strict justice would approve;
But I had rather spare my foe,
And melt his heart with love.

Psalm 121:1. L. M.
Divine protection.

1 Up to the hills I lift mine eyes,
Th' eternal hills beyond the skies;
Thence all her help my soul derives;
There my Almighty refuge lives.

2 He lives, the everlasting God,
That built the world, that spread the flood;
The heavens with all their hosts he made,
And the dark regions of the dead.

3 He guides our feet, he guards our way;
His morning-smiles bless all the day;
He spreads the evening veil, and keeps
The silent hours while Israel sleeps.

4 Israel, a name divinely blest,
May rise secure, securely rest;
Thy holy Guardian's wakeful eyes
Admit no slumber nor surprise.

5 No sun shall smite thy head by day,
Nor the pale moon with sickly ray
Shall blast thy couch; no baleful star
Dart his malignant fire so far.

6 Should earth and hell with malice burn,
Still thou shalt go and still return
Safe in the Lord his heavenly care
Defends thy life from every snare.

7 On thee foul spirits have no power;
And in thy last departing hour
Angels, that trace the airy road,
Shall bear thee homeward to thy God.

Psalm 121:2. C. M.
Preservation by day and night.

1 To heaven I lift my waiting eyes,
There all my hopes are laid:
The Lord that built the earth and skies
Is my perpetual aid.

2 Their feet shall never slide to fall
Whom he designs to keep;
His ear attends the softest call,
His eyes can never sleep.

3 He will sustain our weakest powers
With his almighty arm,
And watch our most unguarded hours
Against surprising harm.

4 Israel, rejoice and rest secure,
Thy keeper is the Lord;
His wakeful eyes employ his power
For thine eternal guard.

5 Nor scorching sun, nor sickly moon,
Shall have his leave to smite;
He shields thy head from burning noon,
From blasting damps at night.

6 He guards thy soul, he keeps thy breath
Where thickest dangers come;
Go and return, secure from death,
Till God commands thee home.

Psalm 121:3. As the 148th Psalm.
God our preserver.

1 Upward I lift mine eyes,
From God is all my aid;
The God that built the skies,
And earth and nature made:
God is the tow'r
To which I fly:
His grace is nigh
In every hour.

2 My feet shall never slide
And fall in fatal snares,
Since God, my guard and guide,
Defends me from my fears:
Those wakeful eyes

That never sleep
Shall Israel keep
When dangers rise.

3 No burning heats by day,
Nor blasts of evening air,
Shall take my health away,
If God be with me there.
Thou art my sun,
And thou my shade,
To guard my head
By night or noon.

4 Hast thou not given thy word
To save my soul from death?
And I can trust my Lord
To keep my mortal breath;
I'll go and come,
Nor fear to die,
Till from on high
Thou call me home.

Psalm 122:1.
Going to church.
1 How did my heart rejoice to hear
My friends devoutly say,
"In Zion let us all appear,
"And keep the solemn day!"

2 I love her gates, I love the road:
The church adorn'd with grace
Stands like a palace built for God,
To shew his milder face.

3 Up to her courts with joys unknown
The holy tribes repair;
The Son of David holds his throne,
And sits in judgment there.

4 He hears our praises and complaints;
And while his awful voice
Divides the sinners from the saints,
We tremble and rejoice.

5 Peace be within this sacred place,
And joy a constant guest!
With holy gifts, and heavenly grace
Be her attendants blest!

6 My soul shall pray for Zion still,
While life or breath remains;
There my best friends, my kindred dwell,
There God my Saviour reigns.

Psalm 122:2. Proper Tune.
Going to church.

1 How pleas'd and blest was I
To hear the people cry,
"Come, let us seek our God to-day!"
Yes, with a cheerful zeal,
We haste to Zion's hill,
And there our vows and honours pay.

2 Zion, thrice happy place,
Adorn'd with wondrous grace,
And walls of strength embrace thee round;
In thee our tribes appear
To pray, and praise, and hear
The sacred gospel's joyful sound.

3 There David's greater Son
Has fix'd his royal throne,
He sits for grace and judgment there;
He bids the saint be glad,
He makes the sinner sad,
And humble souls rejoice with fear.

4 May peace attend thy gate,
And joy within thee wait
To bless the soul of every guest!
The man that seeks thy peace,
And wishes thine increase,
A thousand blessings on him rest!

5 My tongue repeats her vows
"Peace to this sacred house!"
For there my friends and kindred dwell;
And since my glorious God
Makes thee his blest abode,
My soul shall ever love thee well.

Repeat the fourth stanza to complete the Tune.

Psalm 123.
Pleading with submission.

1 O thou whose grace and justice reign
Enthron'd above the skies,
To thee our hearts would tell their pain,
To thee we lift our eyes.

2 As Servants watch their master's hand,
And fear the angry stroke;
Or maids before their mistress stand,
And wait a peaceful look;

3 So for our sins we justly feel
Thy discipline, O God;
Yet wait the gracious moment still,
Till thou remove thy rod.

4 Those that in wealth and pleasure live
Our daily groans deride,
And thy delays of mercy give
Fresh courage to their pride.

5 Our foes insult us, but our hope
In thy compassion lies;
This thought shall bear our spirits up,
That God will not despise.

Psalm 124.
A song for the fifth of November.

1 Had not the Lord, may Israel say,
Had not the Lord maintain'd our side,
When men to make our lives a prey,
Rose like the swelling of the tide;

2 The swelling tide had stopt our breath,
So fiercely did the waters roll,
We had been swallow'd deep in death;
Proud waters had o'erwhelm'd our soul.

3 We leap for joy, we shout and sing,
Who just escap'd the fatal stroke;
So flies the bird with cheerful wing,
When once the fowler's snare is broke.

4 For ever blessed be the Lord,
Who broke the fowler's cursed snare,
Who sav'd us from the murdering sword,
And made our lives and souls his care.

5 Our help is in Jehovah's Name,
Who form'd the earth and built the skies;

He that upholds that wondrous frame
Guards his own church with watchful eyes.

Psalm 125:1. C. M.
The saint's trial and safely.

1 Unshaken as the sacred hill,
And firm as mountains be,
Firm as a rock the soul shall rest
That leans, O Lord, on thee.

2 Not walls nor hills could guard so well
Old Salem's happy ground,
As those eternal arms of love
That every saint surround.

3 While tyrants are a smarting scourge
To drive them near to God,
Divine compassion does allay
The fury of the rod.

4 Deal gently, Lord, with souls sincere,
And lead them safely on
To the bright gates of Paradise,
Where Christ their Lord is gone.

5 But if we trace those crooked ways
That the old serpent drew,
The wrath that drove him first to hell
Shall smite his followers too.

Psalm 125:2. S. M. The saints' trial and safety;
or, Moderated afflictions.

1 Firm and unmov'd are they
That rest their souls on God;
Firm as the mount where David dwelt
Or where the ark abode.

2 As mountains stood to guard
The city's sacred ground,
So God and his almighty love
Embrace his saints around.

3 What tho' the Father's rod
Drop a chastising stroke,
Yet, lest it wound their souls too deep,
Its fury shall be broke.

4 Deal gently, Lord, with those
Whose faith and pious fear,
Whose hope, and love, and every grace
Proclaim their hearts sincere.

5 Nor shall the tyrant's rage
Too long oppress the saint;
The God of Israel will support
His children lest they faint.

6 But if our slavish fear
Will chuse the road to hell,
We must expect our portion there
Where bolder sinners dwell.

Psalm 126:1. L. M.
Surprising deliverance.

1 When God restor'd our captive state,
Joy was our song, and grace our theme;
The grace beyond our hopes so great,
That joy appear'd a painted dream.

2 The scoffer owns thy hand, and pays
Unwilling honours to thy Name;
While we with pleasure shout thy praise,
With cheerful notes thy love proclaim.

3 When we review our dismal fears,
'Twas hard to think they'd vanish so;
With God we left our flowing tears,
He makes our joys like rivers flow.

4 The man that in his furrow'd field
His scatter'd seed with sadness leaves,
Will shout to see the harvest yield
A welcome load of joyful sheaves.

Psalm 126:2. C. M. The joy of a remarkable
conversion; or, Melancholy removed.

1 When God reveal'd his gracious Name,
And chang'd my mournful state,
My rapture seem'd a pleasing dream,
The grace appear'd so great.

2 The world beheld the glorious change,
And did thy hand confess;

My tongue broke out in unknown strains,
And sung surprising grace:

3 "Great is the work," my neighbours cry'd,
And own'd the power divine;
"Great is the work," my heart reply'd,
"And be the glory thine."

4 The Lord can clear the darkest skies,
Can give us day for night,
Make drops of sacred sorrow rise
To rivers of delight.

5 Let those that sow in sadness wait
Till the fair harvest come,
They shall confess their sheaves are great,
And shout the blessings home.

6 Tho' seed lie bury'd long in dust,
It shan't deceive their hope;
The precious grain can ne'er be lost,
For grace insures the crop.

Psalm 127:1. L. M. The blessing of God on the
business and comforts of life.

1 If God succeed not, all the cost
And pains to build the house are lost:
If God the city will not keep,
The watchful guards as well may sleep.

3 What if you rise before the sun,
And work and toil when day is done,
Careful and sparing eat your bread,
To shun that poverty you dread;

3 'Tis all in vain, till God hath blest;
He can make rich, yet give us rest:
Children and friends are blessings too,
If God our sovereign make them so.

4 Happy the man to whom he sends
Obedient children, faithful friends:
How sweet our daily comforts prove
When they are season'd with his love!

Psalm 127:2. C. M.
God all in all.

1 If God to build the house deny,
The builders work in vain;
And towns, without his wakeful eye,
An useless watch maintain.

2 Before the morning beams arise,
Your painful work renew,
And till the stars ascend the skies
Your tiresome toil pursue.

3 Short be your sleep, and coarse your fare;
In vain, till God has blest;
But if his smiles attend your care,
You shall have food and rest.

4 Nor children, relatives, nor friends
Shall real blessings prove,
Nor all the earthly joys he sends,
If sent without his love.

Psalm 128.
Family blessings.

1 O happy man, whose soul is fill'd
With zeal and reverend awe;
His lips to God their honours yield,
His life adorns the law.

2 A careful providence shall stand
And ever guard thy head,
Shall on the labours of thy hand
Its kindly blessings shed.

3 [Thy wife shall be a fruitful vine;
Thy children round thy board,
Each like a plant of honour shine,
And learn to fear the Lord.]

4 The Lord shall thy best hopes fulfil
For months and years to come;
The Lord who dwells on Zion's hill,
Shall send thee blessings home.

5 This is the man whose happy eyes
Shall see his house increase,
Shall see the sinking church arise,
Then leave the world in peace.

Psalm 129.
Persecutors punished.

1 Up from my youth, may Israel say,
Have I been nurs'd in tears;
My griefs were constant as the day,
And tedious as the years.

2 Up from my youth I bore the rage
Of all the sons of strife;
Oft they assail'd my riper age,
But not destroy'd my life.

3 Their cruel plough had torn my flesh
With furrows long and deep,
Hourly they vex my wounds afresh,
Nor let my sorrows sleep.

4 The Lord grew angry on his throne,
And with impartial eye
Measur'd the mischiefs they had done
Then let his arrows fly.

5 How was their insolence surpris'd
To hear his thunders roll!
And all the foes of Zion seiz'd
With horror to the soul.

6 Thus shall the men that hate the saints
Be blasted from the sky;
Their glory fades, their courage faints,
And all their projects die.

7 [What tho' they flourish tall and fair,
They have no root beneath;
Their growth shall perish in despair,
And lie despis'd in death.]

8 [So corn that on the house-top stands
No hope of harvest gives;
The reaper ne'er shall fill his hands,
Nor binder fold the sheaves.

9 It springs and withers on the place:
No traveller bestows
A word of blessing on the grass,
Nor minds it as he goes.]

Psalm 130:1. C. M.
Pardoning grace.

1 Out of the deeps of long distress,
The borders of despair,
I sent my cries to seek thy grace,
My groans to move thine ear.

2 Great God, should thy severer eye,
And thine impartial hand,
Mark and revenge iniquity,
No mortal flesh could stand.

3 But there are pardons with my God
For crimes of high degree;
Thy Son has bought them with his blood
To draw us near to thee.

4 [I wait for thy salvation, Lord,
With strong desires I wait;
My soul, invited by thy word,
Stands watching at thy gate.]

5 [Just as the guards that keep the night
Long for the morning skies,
Watch the first beams of breaking light,
And meet them with their eyes;

6 So waits my soul to see thy grace,
And more intent than they,
Meets the first openings of thy face,
And finds a brighter day.]

7 [Then in the Lord let Israel trust,
Let Israel seek his face;
The Lord is good as well as just,
And plenteous is his grace.

8 There's full redemption at his throne
For sinners long enslav'd;
The great Redeemer is his Son,
And Israel shall be sav'd.]

Psalm 130:2. L. M.
Pardoning grace.

1 From deep distress and troubled thoughts,
To thee, my God, I rais'd my cries;
If thou severely mark our faults,
No flesh can stand before thine eyes.

2 But thou hast built thy throne of grace,
Free to dispense thy pardons there,

That sinners may approach thy face,
And hope and love, as well as fear.

3 As the benighted pilgrims wait,
And long, and wish for breaking day,
So waits my soul before thy gate;
When will my God his face display?

4 My trust is fix'd upon thy word,
Nor shall I trust thy word in vain:
Let mourning souls address the Lord,
And find relief from all their pain.

5 Great is his love, and large his grace,
Thro' the redemption of his Son:
He turns our feet from sinful ways,
And pardons what our hands have done.

Psalm 131.
Humility and submission.

1 Is there ambition in my heart?
Search, gracious God, and see;
Or do I act a haughty part?
Lord, I appeal to thee.

2 I charge my thoughts, be humble still,
And all my carriage mild,
Content, my Father, with thy will,
And quiet as a child.

3 The patient soul, the lowly mind
Shall have a large reward:
Let saints in sorrow lie resign'd,
And trust a faithful Lord.

Psalm 132:1. 5 13-18. L. M. At the settlement
of a church; or, The ordination of a Minister.

1 Where shall we go to seek and find
An habitation for our God,
A dwelling for th' Eternal Mind
Amongst the sons of flesh and blood?

2 The God of Jacob chose the hill
Of Zion for his ancient rest;
And Zion is his dwelling still,
His church is with his presence blest.

3 Here will I fix my gracious throne,
And reign for ever, saith the Lord;
Here shall my power, and love be known,
And blessings shall attend my word.

4 Here will I meet the hungry poor,
And fill their souls with living bread;
Sinners that wait before my door,
With sweet provision shall be fed.

5 Girded with truth and cloth'd with grace,
My priests, my ministers shall shine:
Not Aaron, in his costly dress,
Made an appearance so divine.

6 The saints, unable to contain
Their inward joys shall shout and sing;
The Son of David here shall reign,
And Zion triumph in her King.

7 [Jesus shall see a numerous seed
Born here, t' uphold his glorious Name;
His crown shall flourish on his head,
While all his foes are cloth'd with shame!]

Psalm 132:2. 4 5 7 8 15-17. C. M.
A church established.

1 [No sleep nor slumber to his eyes
Good David would afford,
Till he had found below the skies
A dwelling for the Lord.

2 The Lord in Zion plac'd his Name,
His ark was settled there;
To Zion the whole nation came,
To worship thrice a year.

3 But we have no such lengths to go,
Nor wander far abroad;
Where'er thy saints assemble now,
There is a house for God.]

PAUSE.

4 Arise, O King of Grace, arise,
And enter to thy rest!
Lo! thy church waits, with longing eyes,
Thus to be own'd and blest.

5 Enter with all thy glorious train,
Thy Spirit and thy word;
All that the ark did once contain
Could no such grace afford.

6 Here, mighty God, accept our vows,
Here let thy praise be spread;
Bless the provisions of thy house,
And fill thy poor with bread.

7 Here let the Son of David reign,
Let God's Anointed shine;
Justice and truth his court maintain,
With love and power divine.

8 Here let him hold a lasting throne;
And as his kingdom grows,
Fresh honours shall adorn his crown,
And shame confound his foes.

Psalm 133:1. C. M.
Brotherly love.

1 Lo! what an entertaining sight
Are brethren that agree,
Brethren, whose cheerful hearts unite
In bands of piety!

2 When streams of love from Christ the spring
Descend to every soul,
And heavenly peace, with balmy wing,
Shades and bedews the whole;

3 'Tis like the oil divinely sweet,
On Aaron's reverend head,
The trickling drops perfum'd his feet,
And o'er his garments spread.

4 'Tis pleasant as the morning dews
That fall on Zion's hill,
Where God his mildest glory shews,
And makes his grace distil.

Psalm 133:2. S. M. Communion of saints; or,
Love and worship in a family.

1 Blest are the sons of peace,
Whose hearts and hopes are one,

Whose kind designs to serve and please
Thro' all their actions run.

2 Blest is the pious house
Where seat and friendship meet,
Their songs of praise, their mingled vows
Make their communion sweet.

3 Thus when on Aaron's head
They pour'd the rich perfume,
The oil thro' all his raiment spread,
And pleasure fill'd the room.

4 Thus on the heavenly hills
The saints are blest above,
Where joy like morning dew distils,
And all the air is love.

Psalm 133:3. As the 122nd Psalm.
The blessings of friendship.

1 How pleasant 'tis to see
Kindred and friends agree,
Each in their proper station move,
And each fulfil their part
With sympathizing heart,
In all the cares of life and love!

2 'Tis like the ointment shed
On Aaron's sacred head,
Divinely rich, divinely sweet;
The oil, thro' all the room,
Diffus'd a choice perfume,
Ran thro' his robes, and blest his feet.

3 Like fruitful showers of rain,
That water all the plain,
Descending from the neighbouring hills;
Such streams of pleasure roll
Thro' every friendly soul,
Where love like heavenly dew distils.

Repeat the first stanza to complete the tune.

Psalm 134.
Daily and nightly devotion.

1 Ye that obey th' immortal King,
Attend his holy place,

Bow to the glories of his power,
And bless his wondrous grace;

2 Lift up your hands by morning-light,
And send your souls on high;
Raise your admiring thoughts by night
Above the starry sky.

3 The God of Zion cheers our hearts
With rays of quickening grace;
The God that spread the heavens abroad,
And rules the swelling seas.

Psalm 135:1. 1-4 14 19 21. First Part. L. M.
The church is God's house and care.

1 Praise ye the Lord, exalt his Name,
While in his holy courts ye wait,
Ye saints, that to his house belong,
Or stand attending at his gate.

2 Praise ye the Lord; the Lord is good;
To praise his Name is sweet employ;
Israel he chose of old, and still
His church is his peculiar joy.

3 The Lord himself will judge his saints;
He treats his servants as his friends;
And when he hears their sore complaints,
Repents the sorrows that he sends.

4 Thro' every age the Lord declares
His Name and breaks th' oppressor's rod;
He gives his suffering servants rest,
And will be known th' almighty God.

6 Bless ye the Lord, who taste his love,
People and priests exalt his Name:
Amongst his saints he ever dwells;
His church is his Jerusalem.

Psalm 135:2. 5-12. Second Part. L. M. The
works of creation, providence, redemption of
Israel, and destruction of enemies.

1 Great is the Lord, exalted high
Above all powers and every throne;
Whate'er he please in earth or sea,
Or heaven, or hell, his hand hath done.

2 At his command the vapours rise,
The lightnings flash, the thunders roar;
He pours the rain, he brings the wind,
And tempest from his airy store.

3 'Twas he those dreadful tokens sent,
O Egypt thro' thy stubborn land;
When all thy first-born beasts and men
Fell dead by his avenging hand.

4 What mighty nations, mighty kings,
He slew, and their whole country gave
To Israel, whom his hand redeem'd,
No more to be proud Pharaoh's slave!

5 His power the same, the same his grace,
That saves us from the hosts of hell;
And heaven he gives us to possess,
Whence those apostate angels fell.

Psalm 135:3. C. M.
Praise due to God, not to idols.

1 Awake, ye saints; to praise your King,
Your sweetest passions raise,
Your pious pleasure, while you sing,
Increasing with the praise.

2 Great is the Lord; and works unknown
Are his divine employ;
But still his saints are near his throne,
His treasure and his joy.

3 Heaven, earth, and sea, confess his hand;
He bids the vapours rise;
Lightning and storm at his command
Sweep thro' the sounding skies.

4 All power, that gods or kings have claim'd
Is found with him alone;
But heathen gods should ne'er be nam'd
Where our Jehovah's known.

5 Which of the stocks or stones they trust
Can give them showers of rain?
In vain they worship glittering dust,
And pray to gold in vain.

6 [Their gods have tongues that cannot talk,
Such as their makers gave:

Their feet were ne'er design'd to walk,
Nor hands have power to save.

7 Blind are their eyes, their ears are deaf,
Nor hear when mortals pray;
Mortals, that wait for their relief,
Are blind, and deaf as they.]

8 O Britain, know thy living God,
Serve him with faith and fear;
He makes thy churches his abode,
And claims thine honours there.

Psalm 136:1. C. M. God's wonders of creation,
providence, redemption of Israel, and salvation
of his people.

1 Give thanks to God the sovereign Lord;
His mercies still endure!
And be the King of kings ador'd;
His truth is ever sure.

2 What wonders hath his wisdom done!
How mighty is his hand!
Heaven, earth, and sea, he fram'd alone:
How wide is his command!

3 The sun supplies the day with light;
How bright his counsels shine!
The moon and stars adorn the night;
His works are all divine!

4 [He struck the sons of Egypt dead;
How dreadful is his rod!
And thence with joy his people led:
How gracious is our God!

5 He cleft the swelling sea in two;
His arm is great in might,
And gave the tribes a passage thro';
His power and grace unite.

6 But Pharaoh's army there he drown'd;
How glorious are his ways!
And brought his saints thro' desert ground;
Eternal be his praise.

7 Great monarchs fell beneath his hand,
Victorious is his sword;

While Israel took the promis'd land;
And faithful is his word.]

8 He saw the nations dead in sin;
He felt his pity move:
How sad the state the world was in!
How boundless was his love!

9 He sent to save us from our woe;
His goodness never fails;
From death, and hell, and every foe;
And still his grace prevails.

10 Give thanks to God the heavenly King;
His mercies still endure!
Let the whole earth his praises sing;
His truth is ever sure.

Psalm 136:2. As the 148th Psalm. God's
wonders of creation, providence, redemption of
Israel, and salvation of his people.

1 Give thanks to God most high,
The universal Lord;
The sovereign King of kings;
And be his grace ador'd.
His power and grace
Are still the same;
And let his Name
Have endless praise.

2 How mighty is his hand!
What wonders hath he done!
He form'd the earth and seas,
And spread the heavens alone.
Thy mercy, Lord,
Shall still endure;
And ever sure
Abides thy word.

3 His wisdom fram'd the sun
To crown the day with light;
The moon and twinkling stars
To cheer the darksome night.
His power and grace
Are still the same;
And let his Name
Have endless praise.

4 [He smote the first-born Sons,
The flower of Egypt, dead:
And thence his chosen tribes
With joy and glory led.
Thy mercy, Lord,
Shall still endure;
And ever sure
Abides thy word.

5 His power and lifted rod
Cleft the Red-sea in two:
And for his people made
A wondrous passage thro'.
His power and grace
Are still the same;
And let his Name
Have endless praise.

6 But cruel Pharaoh there
With all his host he drown'd;
And brought his Israel safe
Thro' a long desert ground.
Thy mercy, Lord,
Shall still endure;
And ever sure
Abides thy word.

PAUSE.

The kings of Canaan fell
Beneath his dreadful hand:
While his own servants took
Possession of their land.
His power and grace
Are still the same;
And let his name
Have endless praise.]

8 He saw the nations lie
All perishing in sin,
And pity'd the sad state
The ruin'd world was in.
Thy mercy, Lord,
Shall still endure;
And ever sure
Abides thy word.

9 He sent his only Son
To save us from our woe,
From Satan sin and death,
And every hurtful foe.
His power and grace

Are still the same;
And let his Name
Have endless praise.

10 Give thanks aloud to God,
To God the heavenly King;
And let the spacious earth
His works and glories sing.
Thy mercy, Lord,
Shall still endure;
And ever sure
Abides thy word.

Psalm 136:3. Abridged. L. M. God's wonders of
creation, providence, redemption and salvation.

1 Give to our God immortal praise;
Mercy and truth are all his ways:
'Wonders of grace to God belong,
'Repeat his mercies in your song.'

2 Give to the Lord of lords renown,
The King of kings with glory crown:
'His mercies ever shall endure,
'When' lords and kings are known 'no more.'

3 He built the earth, he spread the sky,
And fix'd the starry lights on high;
'Wonders of grace to God belong,
'Repeat his mercies in your song.'

4 He fills the sun with morning light,
He bids the moon direct the night:
'His mercies ever shall endure,
'When' suns and moons shall shine 'no more.'

5 The Jews he freed from Pharaoh's hand,
And brought them to the promis'd land;
'Wonders of grace to God belong,
'Repeat his mercies in your song.'

6 He saw the Gentiles dead in sin,
And felt his pity work within:
'His mercies ever shall endure,
'When' death and sin shall reign 'no more.'

7 He sent his Son with power to save
From guilt, and darkness, and the grave:
'Wonders of grace to God belong,
'Repeat his mercies in your song.'

8 Thro' this vain world he guides our feet,
And leads us to his heavenly seat:
'His mercies ever shall endure,
'When' this vain world shall be 'no more.'

Psalm 138.
Restoring and preserving grace.

1 [With all my powers of heart and tongue
I'll praise my Maker in my song:
Angels shall hear the notes I raise,
Approve the song, and join the praise.

2 Angels that make thy church their care
Shall witness my devotions there,
While holy zeal directs my eyes
To thy fair temple in the skies.]

3 I'll sing thy truth and mercy, Lord,
I'll sing the wonders of thy word;
Not all thy works and names below
So much thy power and glory show.

4 To God I cry'd when troubles rose;
He heard me, and subdu'd my foes,
He did my rising fears control,
And strength diffus'd thro' all my soul.

5 The God of heaven maintains his state,
Frowns on the proud and scorns the great;
But from his throne descends to see
The sons of humble poverty.

6 Amidst a thousand snares I stand
Upheld and guarded by thy hand;
Thy words my fainting soul revive,
And keep my dying faith alive.

7 Grace will complete what grace begins,
To save from sorrows or from sins;
The work that wisdom undertakes
Eternal mercy ne'er forsakes.

Psalm 139:1. First Part. L. M.
The all-seeing God.

1 Lord, thou hast search'd and seen me thro';
Thine eye commands with piercing view

My rising and my resting hours,
My heart and flesh with all their powers.

2 My thoughts, before they are my own,
Are to my God distinctly known;
He knows the words I mean to speak
Ere from my opening lips they break.

3 Within thy circling power I stand;
On every side I find thy hand:
Awake, asleep, at home, abroad,
I am surrounded still with God.

4 Amazing knowledge, vast and great!
What large extent! what lofty height!
My soul, with all the powers I boast,
Is in the boundless prospect lost.

5 "O may these thoughts possess my breast,
"Where'er I rove where'er I rest!
"Nor let my weaker passions dare
"Consent to sin, for God is there."

PAUSE I.

6 Could I so false, so faithless prove,
To quit thy service and thy love,
Where, Lord, could I thy presence shun,
Or from thy dreadful glory run?

7 If up to heaven I take my flight,
'Tis there thou dwell'st enthron'd in light;
Or dive to hell, there vengeance reigns,
And Satan groans beneath thy chains.

8 If mounted on a morning ray,
I fly beyond the western sea,
Thy swifter hand would first arrive,
And there arrest thy fugitive.

9 Or should I try to shun thy sight
Beneath the spreading veil of night,
One glance of thine, one piercing ray,
Would kindle darkness into day.

10 "O may these thoughts possess my breast,
"Where'er I rove, where'er I rest!
"Nor let my weaker passions dare
"Consent to sin, for God is there."

PAUSE II.

11 The veil of night is no disguise,
No screen from thy all-searching eyes;
Thy hand can seize thy foes as soon,
Thro' midnight shades as blazing noon.

12 Midnight and noon in this agree,
Great God, they're both alike to thee:
Not death can hide what God will spy,
And hell lies naked to his eye.

13 "O may these thoughts possess my breast,
"Where'er I rove where'er I rest!
"Nor let my weaker passions dare
"Consent to sin, for God is there."

Psalm 139:2. Second Part. L. M.
The wonderful formation of man.

1 'Twas from thy hand, my God, I came,
A work of such a curious frame;
In me thy fearful wonders shine,
And each proclaims thy skill divine.

2 Thine eyes did all my limbs survey,
Which yet in dark confusion lay;
Thou saw'st the daily growth they took,
Form'd by the model of thy book.

3 By thee my growing parts were nam'd,
And what thy sovereign counsels fram'd,
(The breathing lungs, the beating heart)
Was copy'd with unerring art.

4 At last, to shew my Maker's name,
God stamp'd his image on my frame,
And in some unknown moment join'd
The finish'd members to the mind.

5 There the young seeds of thought began
And all the passions of the man:
Great God, our infant nature pays
Immortal tribute to thy praise.

PAUSE.

6 Lord, since in my advancing age
I've acted on life's busy stage,
Thy thoughts of love to me surmount
The power of numbers to recount.

7 I could survey the ocean o'er,
And count each sand that makes the shore,
Before my swiftest thoughts could trace
The numerous wonders of thy grace.

8 These on my heart are still impress'd,
With these I give my eyes to rest;
And at my waking hour I find
God and his love possess my mind.

Psalm 139:3. Third Part. L. M. Sincerity
professed, and grace tried; or, The heart-
searching of God.

1 My God, what inward grief I feel
When impious men transgress thy will!
I mourn to hear their lips profane
Take thy tremendous Name in vain.

2 Does not my soul detest and hate
The sons of malice and deceit?
Those that oppose thy laws and thee
I count them enemies to me.

3 Lord, search my soul, try every thought;
Tho' my own heart accuse me not
Of walking in a false disguise,
I beg the trial of thine eyes.

4 Doth secret mischief lurk within?
Do I indulge some unknown sin?
O turn my feet whene'er I stray,
And lead me in thy perfect way.

Psalm 139:4. First Part. C. M.
God is every where.

1 In all my vast concerns with thee
In vain my soul would try
To shun thy presence, Lord, or flee
The notice of thine eye.

2 Thy all-surrounding sight surveys
My rising and my rest,
My public walks, my private ways,
And secrets of my breast.

3 My thoughts lie open to the Lord
Before they're form'd within:

And ere my lips pronounce the word,
He knows the sense I mean.

4 O wondrous knowledge, deep and high!
Where can a creature hide?
Within thy circling arms I lie,
Beset on every side.

5 So let thy grace surround me still,
And like a bulwark prove,
To guard my soul from every ill,
Secur'd by sovereign love.

PAUSE.

6 Lord, where shall guilty souls retire,
Forgotten and unknown?
In hell they meet thy dreadful fire,
In heaven thy glorious throne.

7 Should I suppress my vital breath
To 'scape the wrath divine,
Thy voice would break the bars of death,
And make the grave resign.

8 If wing'd with beams of morning light,
I fly beyond the west,
Thy hand, which must support my flight,
Would soon betray my rest.

9 If o'er my sins I think to draw
The curtains of the night,
Those flaming eyes that guard thy law
Would turn the shades to light.

10 The beams of noon, the midnight hour,
Are both alike to thee:
O may I ne'er provoke that power
From which I cannot flee!

Psalm 139:5. Second Part. C. M.
The wisdom of God in the formation of man.

1 When I with pleasing wonder stand,
And all my frame survey,
Lord, 'tis thy work; I own thy hand
Thus built my humble clay.

2 Thy hand my heart and reins possest
Where unborn nature grew,

Thy wisdom all my features trac'd,
And all my members drew.

3 Thine eye with nicest care survey'd
The growth of every part;
Till the whole scheme thy thoughts had laid
Was copied by thy art.

4 Heaven, earth, and sea, and fire, and wind,
Shew me thy wondrous skill;
But I review myself, and find
Diviner wonders still.

5 Thy awful glories round me shine,
My flesh proclaims thy praise;
Lord, to thy works of nature join
Thy miracles of grace.

Psalm 139:6. 14 17 18. Third Part. C. M.
The mercies of God innumerable.

An evening psalm.

1 Lord, when I count thy mercies o'er,
They strike me with surprise;
Not all the sands that spread the shore
To equal numbers rise.

2 My flesh with fear and wonder stands,
The product of thy skill,
And hourly blessings from thy hands,
Thy thoughts of love reveal.

3 These on my heart by night I keep;
How kind, how dear to me!
O may the hour that ends my sleep
Still find my thoughts with thee.

Psalm 141. 2-5.
Watchfulness, and brotherly reproof.

A morning or evening psalm.

1 My God, accept my early vows,
Like morning incense in thine house,
And let my nightly worship rise
Sweet as the evening sacrifice.

2 Watch o'er my lips, and guard them, Lord,
From every rash and heedless word;
Nor let my feet incline to tread
The guilty path where sinners lead.

3 O may the righteous, when I stray,
Smite, and reprove my wandering way!
Their gentle words, like ointment shed,
Shall never bruise, but cheer my head.

4 When I behold them prest with grief, I'll cry to
heaven for their relief; And by my warm
petitions prove how much I prize their faithful
love.

Psalm 142.
God is the hope of the helpless.

1 To God I made my sorrows known,
From God I sought relief;
In long complaints before his throne
I pour'd out all my grief.

2 My soul was overwhelm'd with woes,
My heart began to break;
My God, who all my burdens knows,
He knows the way I take.

3 On every side I cast mine eye,
And found my helpers gone,
While friends and strangers pass'd me by
Neglected or unknown.

4 Then did I raise a louder cry,
And call'd thy mercy near,
"Thou art my portion when I die,
"Be thou my refuge here."

5 Lord, I am brought exceeding low,
Now let thine ear attend,
And make my foes who vex me know
I've an almighty Friend.

6 From my sad prison set me free,
Then shall I praise thy Name,
And holy men shall join with me
Thy kindness to proclaim.

Psalm 143.
Complaint of heavy afflictions in mind and body.

1 My righteous Judge, my gracious God,
Hear when I spread my hands abroad
And cry for succour from thy throne,
O make thy truth and mercy known.

2 Let judgment not against me pass;
Behold thy servant pleads thy grace:
Should justice call us to thy bar,
No man alive is guiltless there.

3 Look down in pity, Lord, and see
The mighty woes that burden me;
Down to the dust my life is brought,
Like one long bury'd and forgot.

4 I dwell in darkness and unseen,
My heart is desolate within;
My thoughts in musing silence trace
The ancient wonders of thy grace.

5 Thence I derive a glimpse of hope
To bear my sinking spirits up;
I stretch my hands to God again,
And thirst like parched lands for rain.

6 For thee I thirst, I pray, I mourn;
When will thy smiling face return?
Shall all my joys on earth remove?
And God for ever hide his love?

7 My God, thy long delay to save
Will sink thy prisoner to the grave;
My heart grows faint, and dim mine eye;
Make haste to help before I die.

8 The night is witness to my tears,
Distressing pains, distressing fears;
O might I hear thy morning voice,
How would my weary'd powers rejoice!

9 In thee I trust, to thee I sigh,
And lift my heavy soul on high,
For thee sit waiting all the day,
And wear the tiresome hours away.

10 Break off my fetters, Lord, and show
Which is the path my feet should go;

If snares and foes beset the road,
I flee to hide me near my God.

11 Teach me to do thy holy will,
And lead me to thy heavenly hill;
Let the good Spirit of thy love
Conduct me to thy courts above.

12 Then shall my soul no more complain,
The tempter then shall rage in vain;
And flesh that was my foe before,
Shall never vex my spirit more.

Psalm 144:1. 1 2. First Part.
Assistance and victory in the spiritual warfare.

1 For ever blessed be the Lord,
My Saviour and my shield;
He sends his Spirit with his word
To arm me for the field.

2 When sin and hell their force unite,
He makes my soul his care,
Instructs me to the heavenly fight,
And guards me thro' the war.

3 A friend and helper so divine
Doth my weak courage raise;
He makes the glorious victory mine,
And his shall be the praise.

Psalm 144:2. 3 4 5 6. Second Part.
The vanity of man, and condescension of God.

1 Lord, what is man, poor feeble man,
Born of the earth at first!
His life a shadow, light and vain,
Still hasting to the dust.

2 O what is feeble dying man
Or any of his race,
That God should make it his concern
To visit him with grace!

3 That God who darts his lightnings down,
Who shakes the worlds above,
And mountains tremble at his frown,
How wondrous is his love.

Psalm 144:3. 12-15. Third Part.
Grace above riches; or, The happy nation.

1 Happy the city, where their sons
Like pillars round a palace set,
And daughters bright as polish'd stones
Give strength and beauty to the state.

2 Happy the country, where the sheep,
Cattle, and corn, have large increase;
Where men securely work or sleep,
Nor sons of plunder break the peace.

3 Happy the nation thus endow'd,
But more divinely blest are those
On whom the all-sufficient God
Himself with all his grace bestows.

Psalm 145:1. L. M.
The greatness of God.

1 My God, my King, thy various praise
Shall fill the remnant of my days;
Thy grace employ my humble tongue
Till death and glory raise the song.

2 The wings of every hour shall bear
Some thankful tribute to thine ear;
And every setting sun shall see
New works of duty done for thee.

3 Thy truth and justice I'll proclaim;
Thy bounty flows, an endless stream,
Thy mercy swift, thine anger slow,
But dreadful to the stubborn foe.

4 Thy works with sovereign glory shine,
And speak thy majesty divine;
Let Britain round her shores proclaim
The sound and honour of thy Name.

5 Let distant times and nations raise
The long succession of thy praise;
And unborn ages make my song
The joy and labour of their tongue.

6 But who can speak thy wondrous deeds?
Thy greatness all our thoughts exceeds!
Vast and unsearchable thy ways!
Vast and immortal be thy praise!

Psalm 145:2. 1-7 11-13. First Part.
The greatness of God.

1 Long as I live I'll bless thy Name,
My King, my God of love;
My work and joy shall be the same
In the bright world above.

2 Great is the Lord, his power unknown,
And let his praise be great:
I'll sing the honours of thy throne,
Thy works of grace repeat.

3 Thy grace shall dwell upon my tongue;
And while my lips rejoice,
The men that hear my sacred song
Shall join their cheerful voice.

4 Fathers to Sons shall teach thy Name,
And children learn thy ways;
Ages to come thy truth proclaim,
And nations sound thy praise.

5 Thy glorious deeds of ancient date
Shall thro' the world be known;
Thine arm of power, thy heavenly state,
With public splendor shown.

6 The world is manag'd by thy hands,
Thy saints are rul'd by love;
And thine eternal kingdom stands,
Tho' rocks and hills remove.

Psalm 145:3. 7 &c. Second Part.
The goodness of God.

1 Sweet is the memory of thy grace,
My God, my heavenly king;
Let age to age thy righteousness
In sounds of glory sing.

2 God reigns on high, but not confines
His goodness to the skies;
Thro' the whole earth his bounty shines,
And every want supplies.

3 With longing eyes thy creatures wait
On thee for daily food,
Thy liberal hand provides their meat
And fills their mouths with good.

4 How kind are thy compassions, Lord!
How slow thine anger moves!
But soon he sends his pardoning word
To cheer the souls he loves.

5 Creatures, with all their endless race,
Thy power and praise proclaim;
But saints that taste thy richer grace
Delight to bless thy Name.

Psalm 145:4. 14 17 &c. Third Part.
Mercy to sufferers; or, God hearing prayer.

1 Let every tongue thy goodness speak,
Thou sovereign Lord of all;
Thy strengthening hands uphold the weak,
And raise the poor that fall.

2 When sorrow bows the spirit down,
Or virtue lies distrest
Beneath some proud oppressor's frown,
Thou giv'st the mourners rest.

3 The Lord supports our tottering days,
And guides our giddy youth;
Holy and just are all his ways,
And all his words are truth.

4 He knows the pains his servants feel,
He hears his children cry,
And their best wishes to fulfil
His grace is ever nigh.

5 His mercy never shall remove
From men of heart sincere;
He saves the souls whose humble love
Is join'd with holy fear.

6 [His stubborn foes his sword shall slay,
And pierce their hearts with pain;
But none that serve the Lord shall say,
"They sought his aid in vain."]

7 [My lips shall dwell upon his praise,
And spread his fame abroad;
Let all the sons of Adam raise
The honours of their God.]

Psalm 146:1. L. M.
Praise to God for his goodness and truth.

1 Praise ye the Lord, my heart shall join
In work so pleasant, so divine,
Now, while the flesh is mine abode,
And when my soul ascends to God.

2 Praise shall employ my noblest powers,
While immortality endures;
My days of praise shall ne'er be past,
While life and thought and being last.

3 Why should I make a man my trust?
Princes must die and turn to dust;
Their breath departs, their pomp and power
And thoughts, all vanish in an hour.

4 Happy the man whose hopes rely
On Israel's God: he made the sky,
And earth and seas with all their train,
And none shall find his promise vain.

5 His truth for ever stands secure;
He saves th' opprest, he feeds the poor;
He sends the labouring conscience peace,
And grants the prisoner sweet release.

6 The Lord hath eyes to give the blind;
The Lord supports the sinking mind;
He helps the stranger in distress,
The widow and the fatherless.

7 He loves his saints, he knows them well,
But turns the wicked down to hell:
Thy God, O Zion, ever reigns;
Praise him in everlasting strains.

Psalm 146:2. As the 113th Psalm.
Praise to God for his goodness and truth.

1 I'll praise my Maker with my breath;
And when my voice is lost in death
Praise shall employ my nobler powers:
My days of praise shall ne'er he past
While life and thought and being last,
Or immortality endures.

2 Why should I make a man my trust?
Princes must die and turn to dust;

Vain is the help of flesh and blood:
Their breath departs, their pomp and power,
And thoughts all vanish in an hour,
Nor can they make their promise good.

3 Happy the man whose hopes rely
On Israel's God: he made the sky,
And earth and seas with all their train;
His truth for ever stands secure;
He saves th' opprest, he feeds the poor,
And none shall find his promise vain.

4 The Lord hath eyes to give the blind;
The Lord supports the sinking mind;
He sends the labouring conscience peace:
He helps the stranger in distress,
The widow and the fatherless,
And grants the prisoner sweet release.

5 He loves his saints; he knows them well,
But turns the wicked down to hell;
Thy God, O Zion, ever reigns:
Let every tongue, let every age,
In this exalted work engage;
Praise him in everlasting strains.

6 I'll praise him while he lends me breath,
And when my voice is lost in death
Praise shall employ my nobler powers:
My days of praise shall ne'er be past
While life and thought and being last,
Or immortality endures.

Psalm 147:1. First Part.
The divine nature, providence and grace.

1 Praise ye the Lord; 'tis good to raise
Our hearts and voices in his praise;
His nature and his works invite
To make this duty our delight.

2 The Lord builds up Jerusalem,
And gathers nations to his Name:
His mercy melts the stubborn soul,
And makes the broken spirit whole.

3 He form'd the stars, those heavenly flames,
He counts their numbers, calls their names:
His wisdom's vast, and knows no bound,
A deep where all our thoughts are drown'd.

4 Great is our Lord, and great his might;
And all his glories infinite:
He crowns the meek, rewards the just,
And treads the wicked to the dust.

PAUSE.

5 Sing to the Lord, exalt him high,
Who spreads his cloud all round the sky,
There he prepares the fruitful rain,
Nor lets the drops descend in vain.

6 He makes the grass the hills adorn,
And clothes the smiling fields with corn,
The beasts with food his hands supply,
And the young ravens when they cry.

7 What is the creature's skill or force,
The sprightly man, the warlike horse,
The nimble wit, the active limb?
All are too mean delights for him.

8 But saints are lovely in his sight;
He views his children with delight:
He sees their hope, he knows their fear,
And looks and loves his image there.

Psalm 147:2. Second Part.
Summer and winter.

A song for Great Britain.

1 O Britain, praise thy mighty God,
And make his honours known abroad,
He bid the ocean round thee flow;
Not bars of brass could guard thee so.

2 Thy children are secure and blest;
Thy shores have peace, thy cities rest;
He feeds thy sons with finest wheat,
And adds his blessing to their meat.

3 Thy changing season he ordains,
Thine early and thy later rains:
His flakes of snow like wool he sends,
And thus the springing corn defends.

4 With hoary frost he strews the ground;
His hail descends with clattering sound:

Where is the man so vainly bold
That dares defy his dreadful cold?

5 He bids the southern breezes blow,
The ice dissolves, the waters flow;
But he hath nobler works and ways
To call the Britons to his praise.

6 To all the Isle his laws are shown,
His gospel thro' the nation known;
He hath not thus reveal'd his word
To every land: Praise ye the Lord.

Psalm 147:3. 7-9 13-18. C. M.
The seasons of the year.

1 With songs and honours sounding loud
Address the Lord on high;
Over the heavens he spreads his cloud,
And waters veil the sky.

2 He sends his showers of blessing down
To cheer the plains below;
He makes the grass the mountains crown,
And corn in vallies grow.

3 He gives the grazing ox his meat,
He hears the ravens cry;
But man, who tastes his finest wheat,
Should raise his honours high.

4 His steady counsels change the face
Of the declining year;
He bids the sun cut short his race,
And wintry days appear.

5 His hoary frost, his fleecy snow
Descend and clothe the ground;
The liquid streams forbear to flow,
In icy fetters bound.

6 When from his dreadful stores on high
He pours the rattling hail,
The wretch that dares this God defy
Shall find his courage fail.

7 He sends his word and melts the snow,
The fields no longer mourn;
He calls the warmer gales to blow,
And bids the spring return.

8 The changing wind, the flying cloud,
Obey his mighty word:
With songs and honours sounding loud,
Praise ye the sovereign Lord.

Psalm 148:1. P. M.
Praise to God from all creatures.

1 Ye tribes of Adam, join
With heaven, and earth, and seas,
And offer notes divine
To your Creator's praise:
Ye holy throng
Of angels bright,
In worlds of light,
Begin the song.

2 Thou sun with dazzling rays,
And moon that rules the night,
Shine to your Maker's praise,
With stars of twinkling light:
His power declare,
Ye floods on high,
And clouds that fly
In empty air.

3 The shining worlds above
In glorious order stand,
Or in swift courses move
By his supreme command:
He spake the word,
And all their frame
From nothing came
To praise the Lord.

4 He mov'd their mighty wheels
In unknown ages past,
And each his word fulfils
While time and nature last:
In different ways
His works proclaim
His wondrous Name,
And speak his praise.

PAUSE.

5 Let all the earth-born race,
And monsters of the deep,
The fish that cleave the seas,
Or in their bosom sleep,
From sea and shore

Their tribute pay,
And still display
Their Maker's power.

6 Ye vapours, hail, and snow,
Praise ye Th' almighty Lord,
And stormy winds that blow
To execute his word:
When lightnings shine,
Or thunders roar,
Let earth adore
His hand divine.

7 Ye mountains near the skies,
With lofty cedars there,
And trees of humbler size,
That fruit in plenty bear;
Beasts wild and tame,
Birds, flies, and worms,
In various forms
Exalt his Name.

8 Ye kings and judges, fear
The Lord, the sovereign King;
And while you rule us here,
His heavenly honours sing:
Nor let the dream
Of power and state
Make you forget
His power supreme.

9 Virgins, and youths, engage
To sound his praise divine,
While infancy and age
Their feebler voices join:
Wide as he reigns
His Name be sung
By every tongue
In endless strains.

10 Let all the nations fear
The God that rules above;
He brings his people near,
And makes them taste his love:
While earth and sky
Attempt his praise,
His saints shall raise
His honours high.

Psalm 148:2. Paraphrased. L. M.
Universal praise to God.

1 Loud hallelujahs to the Lord,
From distant worlds where creatures dwell:
Let heaven begin the solemn word,
And sound it dreadful down to hell.

Note. This psalm may be sung to the tune of the old 112th or 127th Psalm, if these two lines be added to every stanza, viz.

Each of his works his Name displays,
But they can ne'er fulfil the praise.

Otherwise it must be sung to the usual tunes of the Long Metre.

2 The Lord! how absolute he reigns!
Let every angel bend the knee;
Sing of his love in heavenly strains,
And speak how fierce his terrors be.

3 High on a throne his glories dwell,
An awful throne of shining bliss:
Fly thro' the world, O sun, and tell
How dark thy beams compar'd to his.

4 Awake, ye tempests, and his fame
In sounds of dreadful praise declare;
And the sweet whisper of his Name
Fill every gentler breeze of air.

5 Let clouds, and winds, and waves agree
To join their praise with blazing fire;
Let the firm earth, and rolling sea,
In this eternal song conspire.

6 Ye flowery plains, proclaim his skill;
Vallies, lie low before his eye;
And let his praise from every hill
Rise tuneful to the neighbouring sky.

7 Ye stubborn oaks, and stately pines,
Bend your high branches and adore:
Praise him, ye beasts, in different strains;
The lamb must bleat, the lion roar.

8 Birds, ye must make his praise your theme,
Nature demands a song from you;
While the dumb fish that cut the stream
Leap up, and mean his praises too.

9 Mortals, can you refrain your tongue,
When nature all around you sings?
O for a shout from old and young,
From humble swains, and lofty kings!

10 Wide as his vast dominion lies
Make the Creator's name be known;
Loud as his thunder shout his praise,
And sound it lofty as his throne.

11 Jehovah! 'tis a glorious word,
O may it dwell on every tongue!
But saints who best have known the Lord
Are bound to raise the noblest song.

12 Speak of the wonders of that love
Which Gabriel plays on every chord:
From all below and all above,
Loud hallelujahs to the Lord!

Psalm 148:3. S. M.
Universal praise.

1 Let every creature join
To praise th' eternal God;
Ye heavenly hosts, the song begin,
And sound his Name abroad.

2 Thou sun with golden beams,
And moon with paler rays;
Ye starry lights, ye twinkling flames,
Shine to your Maker's praise.

3 He built those worlds above,
And fix'd their wondrous frame;
By his command they stand or move,
And ever speak his Name.

4 Ye vapours, when ye rise,
Or fall in showers, or snow,
Ye thunders, murmuring round the skies,
His power and glory show.

5 Wind, hail, and flashing fire,
Agree to praise the Lord,
When ye in dreadful storms conspire
To execute his word.

6 By all his works above
His honours be exprest;

But saints that taste his saving love
Should sing his praises best.

PAUSE I.

7 Let earth and ocean know
They owe their Maker praise;
Praise him, ye watery worlds below,
And monsters of the seas.

8 From mountains near the sky
Let his high praise resound,
From humble shrubs and cedars high,
And vales and fields around.

9 Ye lions of the wood,
And tamer beasts that graze,
Ye live upon his daily food,
And he expects your praise.

10 Ye birds of lofty wing,
On high his praises bear;
Or sit on flowery boughs, and sing
Your Maker's glory there.

11 Ye creeping ants and worms,
His various wisdom show,
And flies, in all your shining swarms,
Praise him that drest you so.

12 By all the earth-born race
His honours be exprest;
But saints that know his heavenly grace
Should learn to praise him best.

PAUSE II.

13 Monarchs of wide command,
Praise ye th' eternal King;
Judges, adore that sovereign hand
Whence all your honours spring.

14 Let vigorous youth engage
To sound his praises high;
While growing babes, and withering age,
Their feebler voices try.

15 United zeal be shown,
His wondrous fame to raise;
God is the Lord: his name alone
Deserves our endless praise.

16 Let nature join with art,
And all pronounce him blest;
But saints that dwell so near his heart,
Should sing his praises best.

Psalm 149.
Praise God, all his saints; or,
The saints judging the world.

1 All ye that love the Lord, rejoice,
And let your songs be new;
Amidst the church with cheerful voice
His later wonders shew.

2 The Jews, the people of his grace,
Shall their Redeemer sing;
And Gentile nations join the praise,
While Zion owns her King.

3 The Lord takes pleasure in the just,
Whom sinners treat with scorn;
The meek that lie despis'd in dust
Salvation shall adorn.

4 Saints should be joyful in their King,
Ev'n on a dying bed;
And like the souls in glory sing,
For God shall raise the dead.

5 Then his high praise shall fill their tongues,
Their hands shall wield the sword;
And vengeance shall attend their songs,
The vengeance of the Lord.

6 When Christ his judgment-seat ascends,
And bids the world appear,
Thrones are prepar'd for all his friends,
Who humbly lov'd him here.

7 Then shall they rule with iron rod
Nations that dar'd rebel;
And join the sentence of their God
On tyrants doom'd to hell.

8 The royal sinners bound in chains
New triumphs shall afford;
Such honour for the saints remains:
Praise ye, and love the Lord.

Psalm 150. 1 2 6.

A song of praise.

1 In God's own house pronounce his praise,
His grace he there reveals;
To heaven your joy and wonder raise,
For there his glory dwells.

2 Let all your sacred passions move,
While you rehearse his deeds;
But the great work of saving love
Your highest praise exceeds.

3 All that have motion, life, and breath,
Proclaim your Maker blest;
Yet when my voice expires in death,
My soul shall praise him best.

Doxology.

The Christian Doxology.

Long Metre.

To God the Father, God the Son,
And God the Spirit, Three in One,
Be honour, praise, and glory given,
By all on earth, and all in heaven.

Common Metre.

Let God the Father, and the Son,
And Spirit be ador'd,
Where there are works to make him known,
Or saints to love the Lord.

Common Metre.

Where the tune includes two stanzas.

1 The God of mercy be ador'd,
Who calls our souls from death,
Who saves by his redeeming word,
And new-creating breath.

2 To praise the Father and the Son
And Spirit all divine,
The One in Three, and Three in One,
Let saints and angels join.

Short Metre.

Ye angels round the throne,
And saints that dwell below,
Worship the Father, love the Son,
And bless the Spirit too.

As the 113th Psalm.

Now to the great and sacred Three,
The Father, Son, and Spirit be
Eternal praise and glory given,
Thro' all the worlds where God is known,
By all the angels near the throne,
And all the saints in earth and heaven.

As the 148th Psalm.

To God the Father's throne
Perpetual honours raise,
Glory to God the Son,
To God the Spirit praise:
With all our powers,
Eternal King,
Thy Name we sing,
While faith adores.

Made in the USA
Las Vegas, NV
21 September 2021

30806606R00072